Care Leavers Experiences of Transitioning from 'being in Care' to 'being Independent': Comparing Aspiration to Reality

Steven M. Preston

© Steven M. Preston 2018.

All rights reserved. No reproduction, copy or transmission of this publication may be made without written permission of the author.

No paragraph of this publication may be reproduced, copied or transmitted save with written permission or in accordance with provisions of the Copyright, Designs and Patent Act (1988).

Any person who does any unauthorised act in relation to this publication may be liable to criminal prosecution and civil damages.

The author has asserted their rights to be identified as the author of this work in accordance with the Copyright, Designs and Patents Act (1988).

First published 2018
Independently published
Leeds
W. Yorkshire
United Kingdom

Email: spreston1980@hotmail.co.uk

ISBN-10: 1717765351

ISBN-13: 978-1717765352

This book is also available in the following eBook format:
Kindle ASIN: B07FLHMT7R

Distributed through Amazon

Abstract

Poor outcomes have long been associated with children and young people in care despite them having positive aspirations for their future (NSPCC, 2014). The transition process for Care Leavers towards independence is one of disadvantage and limited life chances (Stein, 2006a). The aim of this study is to compare Care Leavers aspirations to the reality of their situation as they transition from being in care to being independent. The study employs a qualitative methodological approach based on systematic review procedures of existing literature and research which results in five selected studies being utilised for this review. An interpretative analysis allows participants' experiences and voices to remain at the forefront of the study.

Three higher order themes emerge from participants' accounts: *social isolation of Care Leavers, Care Leavers lack the skills ready for independence* and *lack of and inappropriate use of resources for Care Leavers*. The study draws attention to the importance of social inclusion and life skills while raises the need for improved pathway planning to accommodate the needs of Care Leavers during their transition and tailoring specialist services and wider interagency collaboration with a view of allowing them to gradually transition to independent living.

About the Author

Steven M. Preston (BA (Hons), Pg. Cert, MSc, PGCE) is a Senior Social Worker in the field of Children and Family Social Work.

He has held a range of posts in the social care sector and had has been involved in teaching and supporting learners and students to develop their own practice in professional settings.

He is currently undertaking an MA in Advanced Social Work Practice.

Dedicated to: Rosemary Preston and Jacob Hopps Preston

Acknowledgements

First and foremost, I would like to thank the young people and professionals who I work with on a daily basis who have encouraged and inspired me to think about the challenges and discrimination which children Looked After and Care Leavers face in our society.

I am grateful for the support and assistance which I received from Tracy Race in getting me through this project. It was harder than I thought!

Finally, thanks go to my wonderful wife, Giedrė who has had to put up with all the books, journals, articles, notes, pens and scrap paper littered around the house; while talking care of our new born baby boy.

Steven M. Preston

Statement of Confidentiality

It is important that social workers are aware of issues around confidentiality (HCPC, 2017)

It has been ensured that the content of this publication respects confidentiality requirements.

All names have been changed from the original research or deleted to protect identity and promote integrity.

Signed: *S. M. Preston*

Date: June 2018

Contents

	Page Number
Abstract	ii.
About the Author	iii.
Dedication	iv.
Acknowledgements	v.
Statement of Confidentiality	vi.

Chapter One

1.	Introduction	1.
1.1	Key Concepts and Definitions	2.
1.1.1	Young People in Care and the Looked After Child	2.
1.1.2	Leaving Care and Care Leavers	3.
1.1.3	The Pathway Planning Process	5.
1.2	Why Transitions from Care to Independence?	6.
1.2.1	What are the Aspirations of Care Leavers?	7.
1.2.2	The 'End Product'	9.
1.2.3	Children and Young People's Participation in Research	11.
1.3	Where are we now?	12.
1.4	Purpose/aim of the Systematic Review	14.

Chapter Two

2.	Methodology	15.
2.1	The Systematic Review	15.
2.1.1	Search Strategy	15.
2.1.2	Search Terms	16.
2.1.3	Inclusion and Exclusion Criteria	17.
2.1.4	Search Process	17.
2.1.5	Summary of Included Studies	19.
2.2	Qualitative Research Methodology	20.
2.2.1	Critical Appraisal Skills Programme and the Rationale for its Use	21.
2.2.2	Study Selection	22.
2.2.3	Validity Assessment	22.
	2.2.3.1 Screening	23.
	2.2.3.2 Research Design	23.
	2.2.3.3 Recruitment Strategy	23.
	2.2.3.4 Data Collection	24.
	2.2.3.5 Researcher Reflexivity	24.
	2.2.3.6 Ethical Issues	25.
	2.2.3.7 Data Analysis	25.
	2.2.3.8 Findings	26.

		2.2.3.9 Value of the Research	26.
2.2.4	Data Extraction		27.
2.3	Ethical Considerations		27.
2.3.1	Confidentiality and Anonymity		28.
2.3.2	Stage One Ethics		28.
2.3.3	Ethical Approval		28.

Chapter Three

3.	Results	29.
3.1	Theme 1 – Social Isolation of Care Leavers	29.
3.2	Theme 2 – Care Leavers Lack the Skills Ready for Independence	34.
3.3	Theme 3 – Lack of Appropriate and Inconsistent Approaches to the Use of Resources for Care Leavers	36.

Chapter Four

4.	Discussion	41.
4.1	Revisiting the Research Aim	41.
4.2	Research Findings	41.
4.2.1	Social Isolation of Care Leavers	42.
4.2.2	Care Leavers Lack the Skills Ready for Independence	44.

4.2.3	Lack of Appropriate and Inconsistent Approaches to the Use of Resources for Care Leavers	47.
4.3	Reliability and Validity of the Systematic Review	50.
4.4	Limitations of the Systematic Review	51.
4.5	Implications for Practice and Future Research	51.

<u>Chapter Five</u>

5.	Conclusion	53.

<u>Chapter Six</u>

6.	Recommendations	55.
7.	References	57.
8.	Appendices	
	Appendix A. Table of Utilised Studies	74.
	Appendix B. Critical Appraisal Skills Programme (CASP) Tool Kit	81.
	Appendix C. Example of Extracted and Synthesised Data Leading to Sub-Themes and Higher Order Themes	87.

9.   Index   94.

Figures

1.1   Search Terms and Strategy   16.

1.2   The Systematic Review Process   18.

Chapter One

1. Introduction

Making the transition from 'being in care' to 'being independent' can be a challenging time for those who have been accommodated by the local authority (Adley and Jupp Kina, 2017). Listening to Care Leavers experiences is helpful when trying to understand the complexities which they face. Do the aspirations of young people leaving the care system match their reality?

Research tells us that those young people in care are more likely to suffer from poor life chances when compared to the general population. This is true in all areas of life such as, educational attainment, employment prospects, access to health, housing and other services, low levels of community engagement, high levels of interaction with the criminal justice system and becoming young parents themselves (Barn, et al, 2005; Knight, et al, 2006; Stein, 2009; Smith, 2011). Care Leavers are usually on a rapid acceleration to independent living (Stein, 2004) and on what Briggs (2008) described as the *fast track* to adulthood where the outcome is likely to be poverty and social exclusion. The challenges facing these young people are more acute because they are leaving care at an earlier age than most young people leaving home (Kirton, 2007). This is often final where they have no opportunity to return (Stein, 2006b). Making this transition without the correct level of support ultimately leaves Care Leavers feeling isolated and rejected about the realities of being independent and as such they are disadvantaged at the very start of adulthood (Wade, 2008).

Edwards (2012) discovered that 'research in the field of Looked After children and young people has been biased towards collecting quantitative outcome data which have shown to yield significantly more negative findings in contrast to the general population' (p. 6). The National Audit Office produces statistics to that effect highlighting the differences, for example, one in three young people aged 16 or over leave care before their 18th birthday whereas half of other young people who are not in care are still living at home when they are 22 years old. In addition,

40 out of 100 Care Leavers who were 19 did not have a job, did not go to college and were not doing any training whereas only 15 out of 100 other young people not in care who were the same age were in the same position (NAO, 2016).

The qualitative data which has also been collected (Clayden and Stein, 2005; Duncalf, 2010; Morgan, 2012; Hiles, et al, 2014) can offer greater in-depth realities for this cohort group and enable their voices to be heard so change can come about to improve the outcomes for children and young people leaving care. After all, Care Leavers 'know better than anyone else the impact the services they come into contact with have on their lives' (Ellis, 2002, p. 1).

1.1 Key Concepts and Definitions

Children Looked After by the state is a variegated area of social work practice and one which is multifaceted. Attempts to define key concepts are listed below which are pertinent to the study and aims to help orientate the reader.

1.1.1 Young People in Care and the Looked After Child

Children and young people in care are often referred to as *Looked After* by the state (DfES, 2007). This is under the auspicious of the *Children Act* (1989) as defined by *Section* 22, (1) of the act. Local authorities act as *loci parentis* or corporate parent to those children who are Looked After. Their age range can be from birth to 18 years and they can be admitted into care either on a voluntary or compulsory basis through parental agreement or care order respectively.

Children enter the care system for a variety of reasons. The most common being that their families have serious problems which cannot easily be resolved (Cocker and Allain, 2013). Many of the families receive support services but for whatever reason these have not been successful and there is a need for state care. Looked After children have often suffered from some sort of abuse or neglect prior to their care experiences. Nevertheless, no matter how a child enters the Looked After system the local authority has a responsibility to them including a duty to safeguard and promote their welfare as defined in *Section* 22, (3) of the *Children Act* (1989) (O'Loughlin and O'Loughlin, 2012).

Consequently, once a child becomes Looked After the local authority must complete a care plan in conjunction with that child and any other significant people in the child's life; with plans put in place regarding meeting their needs such as, health, education, social, emotional, cultural, religious, and any contact arrangements (Brammer, 2010). Moreover, Looked After children and young people are placed in various types of care settings. The majority being foster care (74%). Other types of settings include being placed for adoption (3%), placement with parents (6%), secure unit, children's homes and semi-independent living accommodation (11%), independent living (4%) and other residential settings (1%)[1]. Temporary accommodation such as bed and breakfast or hotels are not considered appropriate forms of accommodation for children Looked After (LGO, 2013).

1.1.2 Leaving Care and Care Leavers

Leaving care can mean different things to different people, for example, a return home to birth family or those children who are adopted. It could also mean a move to independent living which is likely to mean a change in living arrangements and a change in legal status (Thomas, 2005). Notwithstanding, there appears to be an expectation that young Care Leavers make this this transition often sooner than they are ready at a time in their lives which is also in transition in terms of their own development (Stein, 2012).

---

[1] Statistics adapted from the Department for Education (2017) *Children Looked After in England including (Adoption) Year Ending Report 31 March 2017*. London: DfE.

All adolescents, whether they are in care or not, confront the same development tasks, as changes to their bodies occurs and relationships and sexuality develops. Young people strive for their own identity and emotional maturity as independence looms (Crawford and Walker, 2017). For most young people they have their family to support them, financially, emotionally, and practically. This is not the case for those young people in the care of the local authority; this is replaced with substitute care.

Teenage Care Leavers have their own particular needs and vulnerabilities due to their early childhood and care experiences which makes them susceptible to risk such as, homelessness, unemployment, substance misuse and mental ill-health (Thomas, 2005). Given all of the changes for Care Leavers in a condensed period of time over the leaving care years then it is understandable that things do go awry for them.

The *Children* (Leaving Care) *Act* (2000) was a legislative attempt to improve the support and outcomes for young people leaving care (Brayne and Carr, 2010). The act created an eligibility criteria of being Looked After by a local authority for a period of 13 weeks since the age of 14 and also Looked After at some period while they are 16 or 17. This can also include an aggregate where young people have had a series of short emergency periods of care which amount to 13 weeks (Allard, 2002).

The act created new categories for Care Leavers, those who met the above eligibility criteria whom remained Looked After are *eligible children*, while those who have left care become *relevant children.* Where a young person who is either *eligible* or *relevant* reaches the age of 18 they then become *former relevant* young people until the age of 25 as recently amended by the *Children and Social Work Act* (2017) regardless of whether a young person intends to pursue education/training or not (LGA, 2017).

1.1.3 The Pathway Planning Process

Through the pathway planning process the local authority has a duty to undertake an assessment of need, allocate a Personal Advisor and prepare a pathway plan as directed by the *Care Leavers* (England Regulations) (2010).

All *eligible* and *relevant* young people are entitled to an assessment of need which determines what advice, assistance and support will be provided to them. Any assessment should be in writing ensuring that those involved have access to this document. The assessment of need must be completed within three month of an *eligible* young person becoming 16 (Allard, 2002).

Following an assessment of need a pathway plan must be produced, also in writing, which maps out a clear route for a young person's road to independence. The plan should include information on name, age, and contact details as well as on education, health, accommodation and any contingency planning (Sheldon and MacDonald, 2009; Brammer, 2010). The plan should reflect how it is going to meet the young person's individual needs (Cocker and Allain, 2013). Further to this, the local authority should seek and have regard to the views of the young person and take all reasonable steps to enable them to participate in any meetings with review of the plan every six month or more, if circumstance dictate (Johns, 2017).

The appointment of a Personal Advisor is a statutory requirement under the *Children* (Leaving Care) *Act* (2000). However, there is no prescribed professional qualification needed for this role. Under *Section 3* of the *Children and Social Work Act* (2017) there is a requirement for local authorities to provide a Personal Advisor to Care Leavers up until they reach the age of 25. The role of the Personal Advisor is to advice, assist and befriend; in addition to co-ordinating service provision to meet the needs of the young people. They should support the young person to participate in the preparation of their pathway plan and encourage them to actively be involved in the review of that plan. Furthermore, they should keep informed about a young person's progress and well-being while maintaining clear accurate written records (DoH, 2001).

Where a young person lacks engagement with the pathway planning process this should be clearly documented with steps taken to re-engage them as non-engagement is not reason enough for a local authority not to undertake its duties under law and regulation (Brammer, 2010).

1.2 Why Transitions from Care to Independence?

'It is often assumed that the care system is bound to fail the children it looks after'
(Frost, 2011, pp. 100-101).

There have been many instances were young people have been silenced while in the care of the state (Waterhouse, 2000); with Care Leavers seen as second class citizens, unequal and excluded from society (Leeson, 2007; Loughton, 2011; Slee, 2016). Many Care Leavers making the transition from care to independence have poor behavioural, emotional and social problems (Berridge, et al, 2009) and there is a significant number who have a police caution or conviction, many with drug and alcohol dependency, some who self-harm and a children's service who 'criminalise' young people through their responses to them (Nacro, 2012). For example, the Howard League for Penal Reform (2016) identified that Looked After children are being criminalised at excessively high rates compared to other groups of young people. This approach is damaging and stigmatising with a notion of what Goffman (1963) called 'devaluation' in which individuals are disqualified from social acceptance with a pejorative label applied. Thus leading to discrimination and a reduction in life chances.

Of course, many Care Leavers are aware of this stigma which is attributed to them and are sensitised to it (Driscoll, 2018). This may lead some to internalise that judgement into their own self-identity leading to low self-esteem and a perpetual cycle of poor outcomes (Reed Ltd, 2011). Nevertheless, the social work profession aims to uphold the ideal of social justice with both the International Federation of Social Workers and the International Association of Schools of Social Workers agreeing ethical principles to that effect and supplicating social workers with the responsibility to challenge negative discrimination and promote social justice (IFSW/IASSW, 2012).

According to Stein (2009) the state can deliver positive outcomes for young people as they make their transition from care to independence but there will need to be selective or specialist services as need cannot be met by universal services alone (Höjer and Sjöblom, 2011). Care Leavers are a vulnerable group and their status in society should be acknowledged (Barnardo's, 2013). Leonard (cited in Humphries, 2005, p. 27) argued for a 'guarantee for disempowered groups a chance to speak; asserting responsibility to them who otherwise would have no control over their lives'.

1.2.1 What are the Aspirations of Care Leavers?

The Oxford English Dictionary (2017) gives a simple yet useful definition of the term 'aspiration' as:

> *'A hope or ambition of achieving something'.*

So with this definition in mind what exactly are the aspirations Care Leavers? Firstly, Care Leavers are not a homogenous group and different people will have different aspirations. Nonetheless, there have been several studies and policy initiatives over the years to decipher just that (Social Exclusion Unit, 2003; Stein, 2004; Ofsted, 2009; DCSF, 2010; Tilbury, et al, 2011; Mannay, et al, 2015; Driscoll, 2015). Health matters are seldom on the list of importance for Care Leavers who have little understanding of the health care system (Liabo, et al, 2016). However, in the majority of cases educational attainment remains a high aspiration and the *Aimhigher* Programme (Ofsted, 2009) intended to raise aspirations of Care Leavers to think about further and higher education as an achievable goal while developing easier routes and greater support for them. It is well known that under-achievement in educational attainment has long lasting effects on the employment prospects of Care Leavers and this is reflected in their higher levels of unemployment (Stein, 2012).

Yet, Tilbury, et al, (2011) in their study found that educational/career aspirations were often overlooked due to placement instability despite young people continuing to have this aspiration. Tilbury, et al, go further and note that these aspirations should not come second place for young people but remain a central theme. On the other hand, Driscoll (2015) discovered that many Care Leavers felt that they had to take control over their own lives earlier than expected which impacted on their ability to aim high educationally or professionally as the main focus was their current practical circumstances or the fact that many did not have the confidence to achieve their aspiration (DCSF, 2010).

Despite recent legislation (*Children and Families Act* (2014)) changes which allows Care Leavers to remain in their current foster placement until they are 21, many opt for independence at 18 in preference to the 'Staying Put' initiative. Reasons for this include, not having a good relationship with their carer, liking the idea of their own place, not wanting to be a burden on others or being forced to live independently when their placement breaks down (Driscoll, 2015, p. 16).

In spite of the difficulties which Care Leavers face, Mannay, et al, (2015) established that they have the same aspirations of those young people in the general population. For example, aspiration of having a good job, a good career, financial security, a loving family, and nice home (DCSF, 2010; McDonald, et al, 2011). This is in contrast to Cameron, et al's (2012) study which highlighted that Care Leavers aspirations were much more modest in comparison due to their early history, care experiences, family background and service provision which they had already encountered. This is further supported by Bentley (2013) who argued that young people's abilities often went unrecognised or unfulfilled which impinged on their aspirations and connect to their self-efficacy. For example, a person will not aspire to their goal if they don't feel able to achieve it (Bandura 1977).

Simultaneously, professionals who work alongside Care Leavers also have their own aspirations for them which can impact upon them in both positive and negative ways. Driscoll (2015) noted a change in professional aspiration for young people leaving care over that last decade. Previously, it was apparent that there was low expectations with priority given to developing life skills required for independence over educational or career prospects (Social Exclusion Unit, 2003). This change of aspiration with an emphasis on educational attainment and career prospects is positive, although in some circumstances misplaced.

Many professionals were narrowly defining aspiration by access to university in order to reach high status jobs despite this not always being the most appropriate course of action (Driscoll, 2015). Moreover, there also appears to be a conflict between a young person's own aspirations and those of the professional working with them (ibid). Likewise, within those young people in care there is a difference when comparing those in residential to those in foster care. Cann's (2012) examination of educational experiences of young people highlighted this difference with some of those who are in foster care expressing a desire to attend university while those in residential, there was a pre-occupation of just trying to achieve their GCSE's.

1.2.2 The 'End Product'

So what do we mean by the term 'end product'? For leaving care social work then this is the finished article of a young person from being in care to making the transition to independence. We have seen earlier how Care Leavers have had a disrupted childhood experiencing a myriad of problems from receiving harmful treatment to loss and separation from birth family, to not having a secure base with little love being shown to them, and with many having insecure attachments. Despite these adversities there are still many children and young people who have a positive experience of being cared for by the state but many do not.

Stein (2006b; 2010; 2012) suggested that Care Leavers fall generally into three categories, although they are not fixed but fluid with Care Leavers moving between them as their circumstances change. The first category are those young people 'moving on' successfully from care. These young people would have likely had a stable and secure placement and developed a positive identity within their own family as well as within their foster family. They may well have achieved educational success and their transition from care to independence has been slow and planned; with young people welcoming the challenges which independence brings. The resilience of this group is clear, they have been able to utilise the support available to them; developing their confidence and taking control over their own lives with less reliance on formal services.

The second category are the 'survivors'. These young people have experienced instability and disruption while in care including various placement moves following a response to an incident which resulted in a placement breakdown or ejection from a children's home. They also leave care with little or no educational qualifications. Furthermore, once they have left care they continue to be 'survivors' often through periods of homelessness and unemployment. They are also more likely to be less independent despite having thoughts of self-reliance and having shaped their own lives. Yet, they are dependent on services being provided (Driscoll, 2018).

The third and final category are the 'strugglers', previously referred to as 'victims' in earlier literature. This was changed by Stein due to the negative connotation of the wording and the more optimistic approach for this group of young people (Stein, 2006b). The 'strugglers' were the most damaged and disadvantaged by way of their pre-care experiences and no amount of care can counterbalance that effect. They were more likely to have multiple school and placement moves and unable to form meaningful attachments to others due to their distrust of adults. Their life chances look extremely dismal as they are more likely to be unemployed, homeless, lonely, isolated, suffer from mental health difficulties and with an aftercare service which is unlikely to be able to subsidise their poor start to life (Stein, 2012).

Whichever category a young Care Leaver finds themselves in vulnerabilities exist. Be that as it may, there are different outcomes for those whom 'move on' than for those whom 'survive' and those who 'struggle' and this can relate to the nature of a young person's transition from care (Stein, 2010).

1.2.3 Children and Young People's Participation in Research

Children and young people's involvement in research has traditionally been about *them* rather than them being active agents involved in their own research (Kirk, 2007; Fraser, et al, 2007; Heath, et al, 2009). More recently there has been an emphasis on children and young people being part of the research process and with a children's service adopting the model of the 'Ladder of Participation' (Arnstein, 1969) which promotes participation beyond mere consultation process (Pycroft, et al, 2015). In any event, those children and young people in care may be reluctant to share their experiences as a result of abuse or neglect and being in positions of powerlessness (Cossar, et al, 2013). Moreover, while in care they encounter multiple adults and professionals involved in their lives further impacting on their ability to share their experiences (Cameron and Muggin, 2009) and all of whom are in positions of power over them (Pond, 2011). Social structures, power dynamics and adult-centric processes often marginalise the role and contribution of children (Race and O'Keefe, 2017).

Hitherto, it is important that children and young people's voices remain heard. Not only does this fulfil legal obligations it also empowers them; increasing their self-esteem to be involved in the decision making about their own lives. This inevitably improves services and enhances democracy (Sinclair and Franklin, 2000). Through the *United Nations Convention of the Rights of the Child* (UNCRC, 1991) and the *Children Act* (1989) there has been a growing recognition of the importance of children's rights and their participation in research. This has further been influenced by the reconceptualization of children and childhood (Kirk, 2007). From one which saw children as unreliable and incompetent to make their own decisions (Kellet, et al, 2007) to one of being seen as active agents who can fully participate in issues which affect them (Hill, 1997).

Nevertheless, Winter (2006) in her study concluded that children and young people's voices were often constrained or silent from research. This was further supported by Davey (2010) who found that children were often left with feelings of being belittled, powerless and devalued as their opinion had not been accorded the value which they should have been. In addition, the nature of children and young people's lives in the social, cultural and political context means that they are 'rarely entirely free to decide for themselves whether or not to participate in research. They are surrounded by adult 'gate keepers' controlling researcher's access to them' (Masson, 2007, pp. 45-46).

More to the point is a child's capacity to consent; 16 and 17 years old can give their own consent, as can younger children who are *Gillick* competent. This was decided in the case of *Gillick Vs. W. Norfolk and Wisbech* [1986] which gave due course to a child's understanding over the issue of consent. Any researchers must ensure that information is given in simple, clear language with a child giving valid consent only when he or she understands their involvement in the research (Masson, 2007); and with the researcher constantly rechecking that the child wishes to continue their participation (Mahon, et al, 1996).

Active participation by children and young people in research is important as it provides a different perspective from the adult caregivers and professionals involved and adds to a greater understanding of the needs of this group (Holland, 2009).

1.3 Where are we now?

Approximately 10,000 young people leave care in England each year (HM Gov, 2013). We have seen earlier how children's and young people's voices have been silenced over the years and a lack of understanding of care leaver's needs resulting in a devaluing of their aspirations.

In 2012 the government implemented the Care Leaver's Charter (DfE, 2012) to ensure aspirations were allowed to develop, with local authorities having to act upon these. The government made direct promises to Care Leavers in respect of honouring their identity, believing in young people, listening to their voice, being a champion for them, giving support, finding a home and keeping young people informed. This was followed a year later by the Care Leaver's Strategy (HM Gov,

2013); with its aim to realise Care Leavers aspirations outlining the steps which government are taking to address concerns raised by Care Leavers in relation to education, employment, financial and on-going support, health, housing and the criminal justice system.

What has been clear from Care Leavers is that quite often they felt forced out of their foster placement once they reached their 18th birthday (ibid). In an attempt to reverse this the *Children and Families Act* (2014) placed a duty on local authorities to consider increasing this to the age of 21. This policy initiative is known as *'Staying Put'*, although early indications suggest that it has had limited success (DfE, 2017). More to the point, the provision was not extended to those young people in residential care who must move on whether they want to or not (Nerey, 2016). This is discriminatory to those in residential care who should be given the same opportunity as their counterparts in foster care.

We have seen from the aspirations of Care Leavers that their health needs have traditionally been low on their agenda (Lialbo, et al, 2016). Even though their mental health is usually an area which requires additional support (LGA, 2009). In 2015 government guidance (DfE and DoH, 2015) dictated that there should be an equal emphasis on physical and mental health where Care Leavers do not experience any delays or barriers in accessing support (Bazelgette, et al, 2015). Notwithstanding, there have been cuts in health and social care spending in recent years which have impinged on available provision (Hiles, et al, 2014; Okolosie, 2015).

Smith (2017) in her study found that nearly half of all Care Leavers in England may be suffering from mental health problems and this is impacted by a Child and Adolescent Mental Health Service (CAMHS) cut-off age of 18. This has led to missed opportunities to support young people who are Care Leavers where problems do not simply go away on their 18th birthday.

Regardless of all the recent policy initiatives there remains a lack of integrated long-term support for Care Leavers (Reed, Ltd, 2011; Stein, 2012, Driscoll, 2018). The UK government was heavily criticised for this by the United Nations Committee on the Rights of the Child (UNCoRC, 2016-d). Stating it is 'seriously concerned at the effects that recent fiscal policies and allocation of resources have had and that they are disproportionately affecting children in disadvantaged situations' (CRAE, 2016). There was over 150 recommendations made to the UK government notably avoiding unnecessary changes in placements and not providing sufficient support to Care Leavers (ibid).

In response to such criticism the government ratified the new *Children and Social Work Act* (2017) extending the provision of support to all Care Leavers up to the age of 25 if they wish to receive that support. While this is a welcomed addition to care leaver provision it is clearly politically motivated and reactive rather than trying to understand the developmental milestones which children and young people go through.

Further to this, Barnardo's made the recommendation of implementing a mental health assessment undertaken by a qualified mental health practitioner in to the act, however, this was rejected by the government (Smith, 2017). Another missed opportunity to create a seamless service for Care Leavers.

1.4 Purpose/aim of the Systematic Review

The purpose of this review is to explore how Care Leavers aspirations compare to reality from their experiences of being in care to making the transition to independence. One of the key aims is to capture the voice of the young person which otherwise would not be heard for this vulnerable cohort group. It is hoped that this research will offer a greater insight into the realities for young Care Leavers as they make the transition to adulthood.

Chapter Two

2. Methodology

2.1 The Systematic Review

The systematic review seeks to identify *all* the available evidence with respect to the given theme (Torgerson, 2003). The study's aim was developed after a thorough examination of all the literature available which led to a focussed outcome of gathering and understanding the aspirational voice of Care Leavers and how this compared to their experience of reality as they made their transition from care to independence.

2.1.1 Search strategy

A systematic search of the available literature was undertaken from a range of databases using the *'Discover'* tool on Leeds Beckett University's electronic library between the 25th November 2017 and the 26th November 2017. Databases included *Academic Search Complete*, *Alexander Street Press*, *PsycARTICLES*, *Social Care Online*, *Social Policy & Practice* and *Social Welfare at the British Library* (see Fig 1.1).

A date range of ten years was applied to ensure available evidence remained current. Further searches included the use of the on-line Internet search engine *Google* and *Google Scholar* which revealed further articles useful to the review aim. Moreover, to ensure that all available literature was identified an *Ethos* database search was also conducted to identify and examine the *grey* literature.

2.1.2 Search Terms

Three initial terms were included: 'care leavers', 'aspirations', 'transition to independence'. Subsequent variants of these were added to enable a thorough search of the literature (see Fig 1.1). These searches produced a large number of returns and consequently were combined with 'and'/'or' using Boolean logic. The resulting articles abstracts were examined for their relevance and from these further studies were discovered which provided links to government policy and guidance as well as legislation. Therefore, government websites such as, Legislation.gov, *Ofsted* and the Department for Education were also searched via the *google* search engine.

Fig 1.1 Search Terms and Strategy

Databases Searched	Date Range
Academic Search Complete	2007 - present
Alexander Street Press	2007 - present
Ethos	2007 - present
PsycARTICLES	2007 - present
Sage Journals Online	2007 - present
Social Care Online	2007 - present
Social Policy & Practice	2007 - present
Social Welfare at the British Library	2007 - present
Google.co.uk: https://www.google.co.uk/	
Google Scholar: https://scholar.google.co.uk/	
Criteria: English Language Only	
Search Terms Initial search terms: 'Care Leavers', 'aspirations', 'transitions to independence' Subsequent search terms: 'leaving care', 'care to independence', 'children leaving care', 'young people leaving care', 'aging out of care', 'outcomes for care leavers', 'experiences of care leaver's'	

2.1.3 Inclusion and Exclusion Criteria

As the purpose of the review was to compare Care Leavers aspirations to their experiences of reality when transitioning out of care; qualitative research was deemed to be the most appropriate discourse to address this. The inclusion and exclusion are as follows:

Inclusion Criteria:
 a. Qualitative research
 b. Geographical location restricted to the UK
 c. *Grey* literature studies
 d. A focus on capturing the voice of the Care Leaver as they transition from care to independence

Exclusion Criteria:
 a. Research paper pre-2007
 b. Quantitative research
 c. Non-English language papers
 d. Papers outside of the UK

2.1.4 Search Process

The search of the databases generated 295 returns for the combined search terms used. However, it was discovered from the title articles that many of these could be discarded due to their relation to health matters following discharge from hospital to home, thus not of relevance to this review. Using the inclusion and exclusion criteria an analysis of both the title and abstract reduced this number further to three studies which were found to be of relevance to the review aims. Two studies which also met the inclusion and exclusion criteria came from an online *google* search. (Fig 1.2 gives an overview of the search process.)

Fig 1.2 The Systematic Review Process

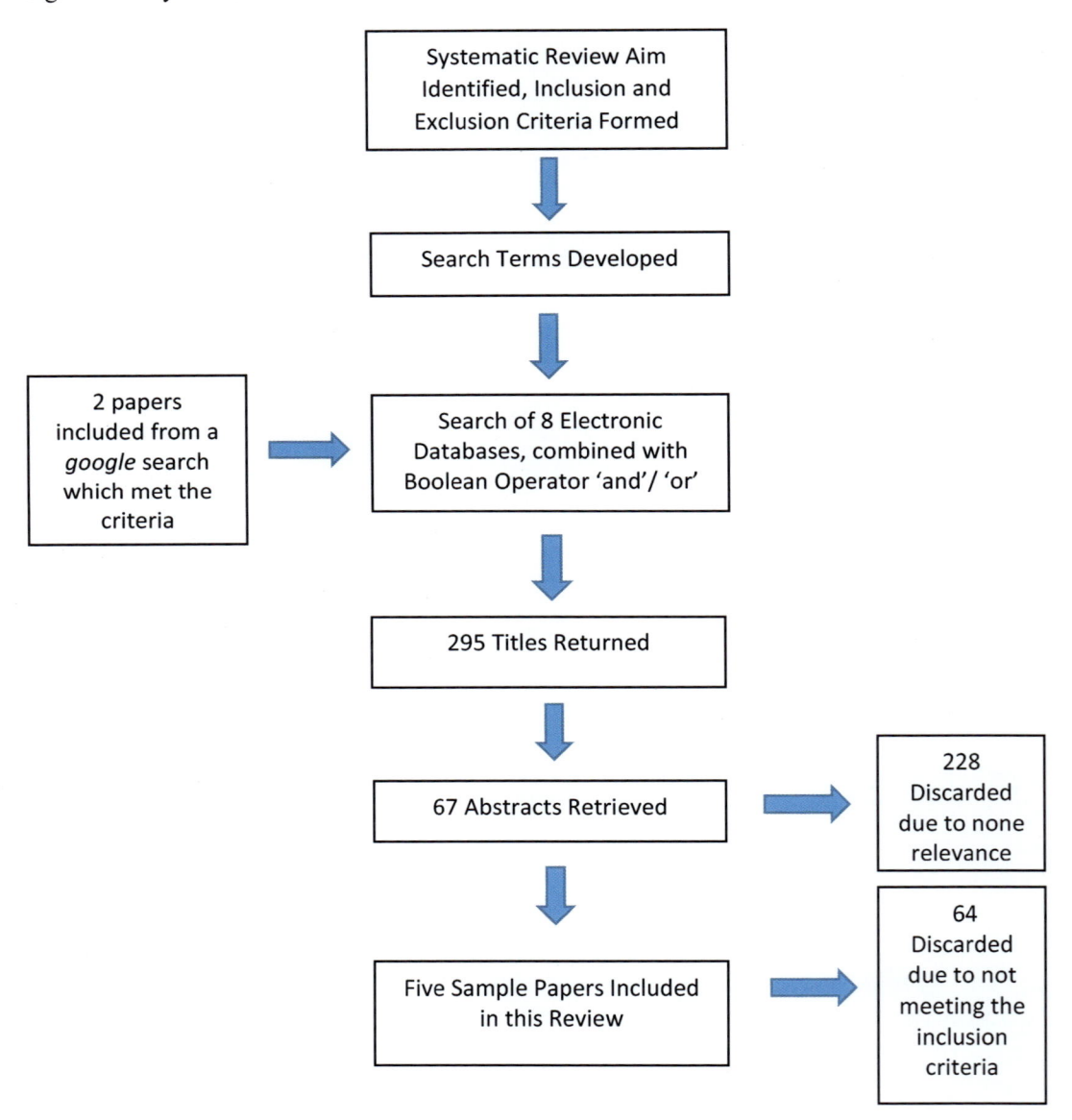

```
┌─────────────────────────────────┐
│ Systematic Review Aim           │
│ Identified, Inclusion and       │
│ Exclusion Criteria Formed       │
└─────────────────────────────────┘
                │
                ▼
┌─────────────────────────────────┐
│ Search Terms Developed          │
└─────────────────────────────────┘
                │
                ▼
┌──────────────────┐      ┌─────────────────────────────────┐
│ 2 papers         │      │ Search of 8 Electronic          │
│ included from a  │ ───▶ │ Databases, combined with        │
│ *google* search  │      │ Boolean Operator 'and'/ 'or'    │
│ which met the    │      └─────────────────────────────────┘
│ criteria         │                      │
└──────────────────┘                      ▼
                          ┌─────────────────────────────────┐
                          │ 295 Titles Returned             │
                          └─────────────────────────────────┘
                                          │
                                          ▼
                          ┌─────────────────────────────────┐        ┌──────────────┐
                          │ 67 Abstracts Retrieved          │ ─────▶ │ 228          │
                          └─────────────────────────────────┘        │ Discarded    │
                                          │                          │ due to none  │
                                          ▼                          │ relevance    │
                                                                     └──────────────┘
                          ┌─────────────────────────────────┐        ┌──────────────┐
                          │ Five Sample Papers Included     │ ─────▶ │ 64           │
                          │ in this Review                  │        │ Discarded    │
                          └─────────────────────────────────┘        │ due to not   │
                                                                     │ meeting the  │
                                                                     │ inclusion    │
                                                                     │ criteria     │
                                                                     └──────────────┘
```

2.1.5 Summary of Included Studies

Five selected studies were found to be of relevance following the inclusion and exclusion criteria. These studies saw the 'voice' of Care Leavers running central to their themes which is of particular importance to the systematic review.

1. Dixon (2008) – This study evidenced the poor physical and mental health of Care Leavers and the instability which many suffered from; along with the limited resources in place to support them.

2. Duncalf (2010) – The study here emphasised what it means to be a young person transitioning from care highlighting the lack of connectedness to others and disabling features which present themselves such as mental health problems and lack of support networks and not being able to reach their full potential.

3. Barnardo's (2013) – This study evidenced multiple moves of placements, homelessness, lack of preparedness and changes in social workers as all impacting on Care Leavers and their aspirations.

4. Hiles, et al (2014) – This study identified the changes in social support and unstable environments for Care Leavers as they transitioned to independence highlighting poor outcomes and feelings of powerlessness.

5. Lushey and Munro (2014) – This research discovered the positive features of peer research and inclusion for promoting aspiration to reduce power imbalances and allow young people's voices to be heard. It emphasised bureaucratic processes on staff which was at the expense of them spending time with young people.

(For more detailed descriptors of the studies see appendix A).

From these studies their relevance is to that of the UK in terms of prominence and context with all the studies undertaken in English. Nevertheless, they are applicable to a European and English-speaking audience.

The results would be of particular interest to those who are currently Looked After or who are Care Leavers, moreover, it may have relevance to those who work with these vulnerable cohort groups. It would also be pertinent to national and local government of the UK and useful to wider society in general.

2.2. Qualitative Research Methodology

Part of the inclusion criteria for the selected studies involved qualitative research. Therefore, on reflection it would seem apt to framework any analysis within a qualitative methodological paradigm and take an epistemological positon as described as Interpretivist (Robson, 2002; McLaughlin, 2007; Carey, 2009). Whereby an 'understanding of the world is through an examination of the interpretation of that world by its participants' (Bryman, 2004, p. 266). Knowledge then is in the mind of the individuals and not something 'out there' waiting to be discovered (McLaughlin, 2007). It is constructed from experiences of the participants (Baden and Major, 2013). With the qualitative researcher attempting to capture that data from the 'inside' using empathetic understanding and attentiveness while 'bracketing off' preconceptions about the topic under discussion (Miles and Huberman, 1994).

To that end, emphasis should be on how this knowledge is constructed in relation to how Care Leavers are perceived rather than any innate features within them. For example, background, context and language will all have an effect on how meaning is achieved in maintaining their interpretation as accurate over the participants they study (McLaughlin, 2007).

2.2.1 Critical Appraisal Skills Programme (CASP) and the Rationale for its Use

The aim of critical appraisal is to form a judgement about whether a selected study has any bearing on a chosen topic and to undertake assessment which results in findings and implications which are reliable and valid (Kiteley and Stogdon, 2014). This is increasingly important because of the vast amount of information available, therefore, researchers attempt to filter out unreliable and lower quality studies (Rees, et al, 2010). This is done through carefully and systematically examining research to judge its trustworthiness, value and relevance (Burls, 2017. Cited in Casey, et al, 2017). It draws together a paper's strengths and limitations while acknowledging that the quality of publications is not always equal (Casey, et al, 2017). Therefore the emphasis is on the *process* rather than the *outcome*.

In order to better support the *process* the Critical Appraisal Skills Programme (CASP) (2017) was realised. This was born out of the need for increased rigorous evidence-based research synthesis (Torgerson, 2003) and was developed by the Oxford University Public Health Resources Unit as a user-friendly tool for analysis (Gough, et al, 2012). Although the tool was initially developed for the health care sector it has been adopted by other disciplines notably the social care sector (ibid). It is available in various forms which are suited to different types of research methods such as, randomised-control trails, cohort studies, case-control studies, systematic reviews, diagnostic-test studies and qualitative studies; it is the latter which has been used to assess the selected studies identified in this systematic review (see appendix B for the CASP criterion for qualitative research).

The use of critical appraisal tools have been strongly recommended by regulatory bodies, professionals and researchers over a long period of time as it is an attempt to be objective and allow for scrutiny of studies (Crombie, 1996; Ajetunmobi, 2002; Aveyard, 2010; Gosall and Gosall, 2009). The Social Care Institute for Excellence (SCIE, 2012) advocates the importance of critical appraisal as a method for research mindedness. Systemically reviewing literature is a complex task and the use of critical appraisal tools such as CASP ensures that all papers are equally and rigorously reviewed appropriately (Aveyard, 2010). Spittlehouse, et al, (2000) discovered in their study the importance of critically appraising research and the use of CASP checklist in particular as a method which is applicable to the social care sector. Moreover, critically appraising research develops critical thinking in professionals which is associated with better decision making in practice settings (Casey, et al, 2017).

2.2.2 Study Selection

The selection of studies used in this review are presumed to be representative of the population of relevant studies based on the systematic review process (Meline, 2006) in the field of care leaver research and capturing the experiences of young people. All of the utilised studies used qualitative data which was appropriate for the research aims of understanding the experiences of care leavers transitioning out of care into adulthood and independence.

2.2.3 Validity Assessment

The current review sought to use the CASP toolkit as a validity assessment for judging the quality of the selected studies used. The application of the CASP toolkit enabled the research to be rigorously checked against a well-respected form of analysis (Akobeng, 2005; CRD, 2008). Using this method helped to ascertain if the selected studies were valid and of relevance, facilitating judgments to be formed which measured whether the studies were robust enough to contribute to the area of investigation (Aveyard, 2010). The following topics were analysed in relation to the selected studies:-

2.2.3.1 Screening

Each of the studies went through initial screening questions with the authors providing a clear statement of aim for their research which is relevant to the current literature on care leavers transitioning to independence. The use of qualitative methodology was an appropriate discourse to address the research aims as it sought to interpret the subjective experiences of the participants of the research.

2.2.3.2 Research Design

Research design was applicable to all the selected studies with justification being provided. However, four of the selected studies (Dixon, 2008; Duncalf, 2010; Hiles, et al, 2014; Lushey and Munro, 2014) provided in-depth descriptions and rationale for their design methodology when compared to the Barnardo's study which appeared to be less informative.

2.2.3.3 Recruitment Strategy

Four of the studies (Dixon, 2008; Duncalf, 2010; Hiles, et al, 2014; Lushey and Munro, 2014) provided appropriate recruitment strategies for the aims of the research. Albeit, Dixon (2008) made reference to a previous study reciting their recruitment strategy while accessing and extrapolating their data (Dixon, et, al, 2006). The Barnardo's study offered no explanation or rationale for their recruitment strategy other than a vague connection that participants were in fact, Care Leavers. Moreover, Duncalf's (2010) study offered a detailed account to the representativeness of the sample. While Lushey and Munro (2014) suggested reasons for the high dropout rate of their participants.

The identification of participants in all cases was through services whom supported care leavers whether that was the local authority or charitable organisations. This made the samples purposive in nature.

2.2.3.4 Data Collection

All of the research attempted to capture the voice of the participants involved using various data collection methods, such as, focus groups, interviews and questionnaires. Exclusively, Lushey and Munro (2014) went further using participatory methods to empower young people and 'democratise both research and social work itself' (Parton and Kirk, 2010). Whereas Duncalf (2010) was the only author to discuss saturation point who felt that he had received a sufficiently high enough response rate to cease his research. In addition, he and Dixon (2008) also collected quantitative data as well as qualitative information to support their claims.

2.2.3.5 Researcher Reflexivity

Researcher reflexivity was minimal or non-existent in most of the studies (Dixon, 2008; Duncalf, 2010; Barnardo's, 2013) with the exception of Lushey and Munro (2014) who extensively analysed bias in terms of the peer-researchers they employed but failed to analyse their own bias which maybe present as they supported the peer-researchers through the project. Duncalf (2010), however, did refer to his own personal experience of growing in care and saw this as a positive in terms of his interpretation of the research. On the contrary this could in fact skew the data and bias any results (Dwyer and Buckle, 2009). More to the point Hiles, et al, (2014) places emphasis on his own transition from adolescence and illustrates the connections he makes to care leavers and their transition; while trying to develop his own identity in the midst of changes in his own life. In spite of this, he leaves it up to the reader to form a judgement as to the extent of any influence that may be present.

2.2.3.6 Ethical Issues

Two of the studies made no reference to ethical issues (Dixon, 2008; Barnardo's 2013) with remarks to ethical approval being granted in Hiles, et al's, (2014) study. Duncalf (2010) discussed the need for anonymity of participants and followed ethical guidelines. Lushey and Munro (2014) were the most extensive in their assessment of ethical issues but in relation to the peer-researchers. There was reference to providing written information on what involvement would entail, support offered, the holding of training events and carrying out criminal records checks. They further discussed safety mechanisms, power imbalances alongside the potential effects of the researchers past and present experiences and whether their study was approved by their university ethics committee.

2.2.3.7 Data Analysis

All selected studies provided supporting quotations to substantiate their findings and capture the voice Care Leavers. Both Dixon (2008) and Duncalf (2010) further embarked on quantification of the data to support their findings and data analysis. Hiles, et al, (2014) was clear in their use of action research to frame their thematic analysis with supportive visual diagrams and the use of qualitative data computer software packages. Poor levels of reflexivity certainly impacted upon the overall quality of the studies as the majority of the researchers failed to address their personal influences on the data being analysed.

2.2.3.8 Findings

The selected studies all had clear findings to the original research question with most (Duncalf, 2010; Barnardo's, 2013; Lushey and Munro, 2014) concluding that care leavers participation and involvement in research should be promoted and recognised the frustration that their voice was not always heard when implementing policy and practice. There was mention of triangulation in two of the studies but these failed to go into any detail (Hiles, et al, 2014; Dixon, 2008). For the most part Dixon (2008) was reliant upon previous research and Hiles, et al, (2014) reported multiple perspectives and independent analysis.

2.2.3.9 Value of the Research

The value of the research was variable as it was clear that both Barnardo's (2013) and Duncalf (2010); on behalf of the Care Leavers Association had aims to either promote their own service or to lobby government. Neither mention if their research was sufficiently scrutinised or independently analysed. With regards to Dixon (2008), Hiles, et al, (2014) and Lushey and Munro (2014) they are all academic university-based researchers who subject their studies for peer-review scrutiny for acceptance and ultimately publication. Furthermore, there is evidence of formal methodologies being used which included, action research, thematic analysis, ethnographical and peer-research methodology.

It should be noted, however, that Dixon (2008) and Hiles, et al, (2014) made little attempt to include ethical considerations into their write-ups making it unclear as the extent of their ethical standards. This could cause doubt as to the overall quality of research and also of the journal in which it was published as publication ethics dictate that informed consent of participants is a requirement which should be sought by any reviewers and the journal (COPE, 2017). Notwithstanding, all the studies highlighted the need for additional help and change in the provision of services for care leavers making findings transferable across policy and practice.

2.2.4 Data Extraction

There is no one process of data extraction from qualitative research (Battany-Saltikov, 2012). Due to the nature of the review purpose, manual data extraction was used. Data extraction generally followed the principles as defined by Burnard's (1991) method of thematic analysis. The aim was to manually highlight data using a colour-coded system based on the following areas:
- Aspirational voice of Care Leavers – red.
- Realities of being independent – blue.
- The system currently in place to support Care Leavers – green.

From here sub-themes were freely generated using open coding and then grouped together to create 'higher order' headings (ibid). This removed duplicate themes and created a revised list of main themes based on the synthesis of the selected studies. Following good practice guidelines; records were stored in wallets alongside the study articles (Gough, et al, 2012).

See appendix C for examples of extracted and synthesised data leading to sub-themes and higher order themes.

2.3 Ethical Considerations

Leeds Beckett University's *Research Ethics Policy* (2017) was adhered to during the completion of this project and the procedures laid down with it were strictly followed. As the university is a signatory to the Concordat of Research Integrity (Universities UK, 2012) accompaniment was also applied to the principles contained with it.

As the author of this review is a qualified and registered social worker in England there is an obligation to adhere to the *Standards of Conduct, Performance and Ethics* of the Health and Care Professions Council (HCPC, 2016).

2.3.1 Confidentiality and Anonymity

The confidentiality and anonymity of the participants was adhered to in accordance with the previous procedures and codes of conduct as mentioned above. There will be no reference of any identifying characteristics or geographical location indicators to protect the identity of participants who took part in the research studies. Any names in this review are pseudonyms.

2.3.2 Stage One Ethics

In the first instance there is a requirement for completion of the university's risk checklist. The risk checklist allowed for risk classification categories from one to three dependant on the given answers to the posed questions. This review was categorised as risk level one which is the lowest classification level available. The checklist is then referred to the Local Research Ethics Coordinator for approval.

2.3.3 Ethical Approval

This research has been approved by the Director of Studies Professor Nick Frost of the Faculty of Health and Social Sciences at Leeds Beckett University on the 9th November 2017 as meeting the requirements for risk classification category one.

Chapter Three

3. Results

The results section presents an analysis of the synthesised studies used; coupled with ascribed Interpretivist methodology as outlined in chapter 2, sub-section 2.2; with three higher order themes emerging:

1. Social isolation of Care Leavers.
2. Care Leavers lack the skills ready for independence.
3. Lack of appropriate and inconsistent approaches to the use of resources for Care Leavers.

Each of the themes will be described in detail with supporting extracts providing illustration. In some cases additional text has been added to improve the overall readability and this is depicted within square brackets [ ]. Moreover, shortened extracts are distinguished by an ellipsis (…).

The main focus of the analysis was to ensure that the voice of care leavers was heard; whom might otherwise have remained silent. After all, Britzman (1989) argued that 'a commitment to voice attests to the right of speaking and being represented'. Albeit, there is an awareness that any approach to *hearing the voice* will involve the selection and editing of data. (Fine, 2002).

3.1 Theme 1 - Social Isolation of Care Leavers

Social isolation of care leavers was prevalent within all the analysed studies. It was clear that many felt 'lonely' and 'isolated' once they had left the secure base of a foster placement or residential care and were living independently.

> "I have just been a bit lonely and down…since I've had this flat. I've had lots of time on my own thinking about not being with anyone and missing things"
>
> (Jade, Care Leaver cited in Dixon, 2008, p. 212)

Jade's description of her current situation was not uncommon for Care Leavers living alone. For many the effects of social isolation can be damaging trigging mental ill-health or poor emotional well-being as Sarah pointed out:

> "If I am alone [for] to long I self-harm and think about suicide and stuff"
>
> (Sarah, Care Leaver cited in Barnardo's, 2013, p. 8)

While Callum stated:

> "I was suffering really bad with depression and anxiety…I was so down"
>
> (Callum, Care Leaver cited in Barnardo's, 2013, p. 7)

Hiles, et al, (2014) in their researcher reflexivity suggested that:

> "Post-care living could trigger or intensify past emotional issues which in turn affect health and coping strategies"
>
> (Researcher Reflection)

What is more, is that these affects can be life-long and life-limiting as one older care leaver purported:

> "I have agoraphobia and social difficulties which have led to serious mental health problems"
>
> (Simon, Care Leaver cited in Duncalf, 2010, p. 21)

Social isolation is not just about care leavers living alone but also about being and feeling alone.

> "Not nice, I was homeless, unemployed, very hungry, very lonely and scared of the future and present"
>
> (Megan, Care Leaver cited in Duncalf, 2010, p. 30)

Megan's emotive language makes it clear in her voice the despair and powerlessness which is often omnipresent with young people leaving care as they can feel that they have a lack of control over their lives. This also includes the timing of when and how they leave care.

> "The day of your 18th birthday, they will kick you out"
>
> (Samuel, Care Leaver cited in Barnardo's, 2013, p. 4)

Being independent does not always match young people's expectations with many finding it extremely difficult to cope alone, wishing that they remained in their previous placements.

> "I'd rather be back in care"
>
> (John, Care Leaver cited in Lushey and Munro, 2014, p. 17)

Weak support networks can further compound the effects of social isolation.

> "If I had my parents to go to, I would go to my parents and ask for their help. Or I'd stay with parents so the strain wouldn't be so much. But I don't have anybody to turn to"
>
> (Liam, Care Leaver cited in Barnardo's, 2013, p. 1)

Care Leavers agree that having someone in their lives who actually cared about them would help them to make a smoother transition to independence and would certainly be a protective factor for them in terms of support networks.

> "[you want] someone being there for you"
>
> (Vicky, Care Leaver cited in Hiles, et al, 2014, p. 6)

> "the best help would be for someone to talk to… I would love that"
>
> (Jo, Care Leaver cited in Barnardo's, 2013, p. 6)

Nevertheless, some self-isolate or had lost contact with those who are important to them such as, previous foster carers, as one care leaver divulged:

> "I haven't spoken to [my old foster carer] for about a year"
> (Brandan, Care Leaver cited in Lushey and Munro, 2014, p. 17)

Reasons for this include:

> "not [wanting to be] a burden to anyone"
> (Brandan, Care Leaver cited in Duncalf, 2010, p. 24)

In addition, there is the constantly changing social network which exists for some care leavers.

> "People have different social networks for doing different things, like some people obviously will have their friends who will go out drinking with them because all do the same thing and they'll have a laugh together …and then they'll have, like another group of friends, like, where they maybe go to college together"
> (Sally, Care Leaver cited Hiles, et al, 2014, p. 5)

Some young people attempted to overcome their social isolation through occupying their time through various means, whether this was socially acceptable or not and on occasions could involve activities which bring them into contact with the criminal justice system.

> "I try to keep my day and night busy 24/7. It is hard but I get by"
> (Sarah, Care Leaver cited in Barnardo's, 2013, p. 8)

> "I ended up shop lifting"
> (Claire, Care Leaver cited in Duncalf, 2010, p. 30)

A reduction in social isolation could come through employment as not only would this offer a source of income it would bring stability to a young person's life, although many care leavers found it difficult to gain employment.

> "[you want] to be given a chance [for a job]"
> (Ash, Care Leaver cited Lushey and Munro, 2014)

Following education aspirations can further help reduce social isolation as this can give care leavers a sense of self-worth. However, coming up against barriers often added additional stress to them when they were already in a period of transition in their lives.

> "I wanted to go to college when I left school but was told I had to get a job and move out"
> (Craig, Care Leaver cited in Duncalf, 2010, p. 31)

> "A university grant of 33 weeks and I had to make it last 52 weeks…
> I was unable to live in Halls and I had to find accommodation that wasn't going to turf me out during the holidays"
> (Louise, Care Leaver cited in Duncalf, 2010, p. 29)

Being unable to pursue leisure activities increased social isolation, with many care leavers linking this to lack of financial resources and using what little money they had available to pay for everyday items such as, food or utilities.

> "when I am at home I try to use [as] little [gas] as possible [in order to save money]. [With regards to] the electricity I don't know how much I'm using"
> (Chelsey, Care Leaver cited in Barnardo's, 2013, p. 10)

There appears to be a many factors in the concept of social isolation for Care Leavers as they make their transition to independence. Not least the difficulties which they are presented with at such a young age. Ameliorating feelings of loneliness is complex and social isolation should not be viewed in isolation but accompanied by our next two themes to offer greater insights into the difficulties which Care Leavers face when transitioning out of care.

3.2 Theme 2 - Care Leavers Lack the Skills Ready for Independence

It was apparent that there is an emphasis on Care Leavers gaining the skills ready for independence. This mainly came around their 16th and 18th birthdays; as pathway plans geared young people through the care system towards independence as Samuel discovered:

> "Once you're 16 you move out of your foster home and then semi-independent… and then you're 18, leaving care"
> (Samuel, Care Leaver cited in Barnardo's, 2013, p. 4)

These traditional milestone birthdays often emulated the ridged nature of the care system with Social Workers and Personal Advisors continuously encouraging and assessing Care Leavers' skills ready for independence as they made their way from foster or residential care to semi-independent living then onto full independence and being responsible for maintaining their own tenancy, being liable for council tax and ensuring that they have the skills to budget for food and utilities. More often than not, many Care Leavers lacked these skills.

> "Yeah, I hated living on my own. I couldn't cope at first…I didn't know how to pay bills or council tax. I didn't know what the letters meant when they came through the post"
> (Bethany, Care Leaver cited in Barnardo's, 2013, p. 8)

Yet, the care system is there to ensure children and young people are appropriately looked after and prepared for adulthood. Per contra, one Care Leaver remarked:

> "[It is evident that there is a] lack of preparation for what happens after care"
> (Dale, Care Leaver cited in Duncalf, 2010, p. 29)

While a professional saw the situation as akin to a 'train wreck':

> "It's like a train wreck…yes, it's like a train wreck, suddenly at 18.
> I definitely articulate that to young people as best I can and say
> you might be kicking against us right now but at 18 it will be most
> likely quite a different world"
> (Dianne, Professional cited in Hiles, et al, 2014, p. 6)

Professionals taking this stance can result in unnecessary pressure or even fear for young people as there is an inappropriate push for independence into an equally inappropriate position of uncertainty.

Moreover, Care Leavers can also be confused about their own status and stage of development which they are expected to be at. The term 'Care Leaver' can itself bring additional pressure for many as they are often informed that they are now a 'Care Leaver' at 16, yet, many remain in care as a Looked After Child until they are 18. This confusing and contradictory message can impact on their sense of identity and their ability to be ready for independence.

> "I was always called a Care Leaver from the age of 16 upwards anyway,
> so it was like, so what I am? I'm a Care Leaver all between 16 and 21
> but I'm still in care, so how come I'm a Care Leaver"
> (Nicole, Care Leaver cited in Hiles, et al, 2014, p. 5)

Care Leavers themselves concluded that in order to gain the skills necessary for independence then they should undertake preparation courses before leaving care.

> "There should be a preparation course prior to leaving care on
> everyday living, relationships, budgeting, self-esteem and the like"
> (Paul, Care Leaver cited in Duncalf, 2010, p. 29)

This could be a potential way forward for local authorities to consider such courses and formal accreditation could increase the sense of achievement, self-worth and efficacy of any programmes.

This was further complimented by the need "to have a role model" whereby young people's views can be shaped in ways which instil good morals and values. Taking a shared approach to learning new skills can help young people develop their self-esteem and gain the skills ready for independence.

> "I'm (Ellie's)...worker but she's teaching me the culinary skills,
> because you're such a good cook, aren't you? You showed me how
> to make soup, last week. So it's about learning from each other as well.
> Even though we're staff, we learn from the young people, it's about
> working together as a team"
> (Dawn, Professional cited in Barnardo's, 2013, p. 11)

Withal, Care Leavers feel that it's not just about the soft skills which they want to develop as Richard envisaged:

> "[Care Leavers] should come out of care with a skill to trade to equip
> them to enter the world of work"
> (Richard, Care Leaver cited in Duncalf, 2010, p. 29)

Up-skilling young Care Leavers with employability competencies is an occurring practice through further education, work placements schemes and apprenticeships. These can prepare them with the skills ready for the workforce. However, for those who do manage to develop the skills required further barriers still exist due to the lack of appropriate and inconsistent approaches to the use of resources available, as our third theme highlights.

3.3 Theme 3 - Lack of Appropriate and Inconsistent Approaches to the Use of Resources for Care Leavers

Lack of appropriate or inconsistent approaches to the use of resources for Care Leavers was reported in all utilised studies. This was mainly around accommodation needs and the use of unsuitable or poor quality housing. Despite statutory guidance, regarding placing any Looked After child or Care Leavers in bed and breakfast or hostel accommodation as unsuitable it remains the case that this is still ongoing practice and often where residents age is not consistent with placed care leavers and where there is use of illegal substances and antisocial or threatening behaviour occurring.

One researcher argued that:

> "Poor housing can affect a young person's health and in turn damage their coping strategies"
> (Researcher Reflection cited in Dixon, 2008, p. 214)

While they further found that:

> "Poor housing situations, being unemployed and lacking supporting networks had allowed [a young person] to dwell on childhood experiences"
> (Researcher Reflection cited in Dixon, 2018, p. 211)

This was further compounded with findings suggesting that:

> "Housing instability, homelessness, unemployment and living on limited financial resources…after leaving care, all of which could impact on general health"
> (Researcher Reflection cited in Hiles, et al, 2014)

Be that as it may, it was often the case in various social care offices that social care staff, who were untrained in health matters were the ones attempting to assist young people but came up against barriers to support them. Highlighting the lack of resources in accessing mental health services as well as the lack of integration between Social Care and Health; as a Social Worker and Team Manager highlighted:

> "We are the people who counselled him and we're not equipped in that department"
>> (Angela, Social Worker cited in Dixon, 2008, p. 214)

> "locally CAMHS is very restrictive…there isn't anything local that is tailor made for young people"
>> (Michael, Team Manager cited in Dixon, 2008, p. 214)

Aside from the housing situation and the effects on health the lack of support is also a risk factor for many Care Leavers.

> "[Some young people moved] on their 18th birthday…from busy children's homes or foster families to a 'dingy' flat…and expected to manage on their own"
>> (Researcher Reflection cited in Barnardo's, 2013, p. 7)

This resulted in Care Leavers struggling with core aspects of day to day living because of the lack of regular and consistent guidance from adults which a parent would naturally give.

> "adult support comes from often selected support workers with caseload ranging between 15 and 40 young people"
>> (Researcher Finding cited in Barnardo's, 2013, p .5)

These widespread difference between staff caseloads and approaches can give different young people very different experiences of after-care support.

> "my worker, he just gets you up, just like that. He just really got my confidence"
>> (Callum, Care Leaver cited in Barnardo's, 2013, p. 7)

> "my main issue is of what I am going through right now, I have left the care system this year in January. I rang up my social worker to talk and she said she wasn't on the team anymore. She gave me another number for the team in [somewhere else]. I spoke to another lady who

> said she was my new care leaver worker and that we should meet up for a coffee. It's August. Enough said I think. The point I am trying to make is yes we are adults, but we still need help!"
>
> (Jason, Care Leaver cited in Duncalf, 2010, p. 31)

> "We set-up the Wednesday evening group and they got benefit from just coming and having a chat and interacting with each other. We do cook-and-eat"
>
> (Kat, Professional cited in Barnardo's, 2013, p. 8)

There was even findings that one social care office opened its doors on Christmas Day for any Care Leaver who wanted to help prepare and share Christmas lunch as a group rather than on their own. Further to this, Joanne (a Care Leaver) was encouraged by staff to take part in the Care Leaver's Forum. This built her confidence until, at 21, she was the Chair. This community participation enabled Joanne to build her confidence and increase her self-esteem which resulted in other young people being snowballed into the event. Findings suggest that young people who have positive experiences such as good quality housing, career participation and good support can improve overall mental health and well-being.

On the other hand, some social care services found themselves being reactive to certain situations mirroring the service users they supported, as Sharon pointed out:

> "Social services are modelling the client…we are responding the chaos and reacting"
>
> (Sharon, Professional cited in Hiles, et al, 2014, p. 7)

This was often done through what Ryan (a Care Leaver) described as "forced or pointless support" (ibid) whereby the support on offer was something which was given not negotiated and where the young person wishes were not listen too.

With professionals counter reacting with responses of:

> "he won't accept the support he needs"
> (Alan, Professional cited in Dixon, 2008, p. 214)

This highlights the complex way in which Social Care systems are setup and resourced as they respond to crisis situations which can leave those who are not in crisis to be left without support in which they are entitled to.

Moreover, some Care Leavers reported the bureaucratic way in which staff completed their pathway plans leading to less quality time with their workers:

> "[Staff] spend too much time on paperwork…we call it the pathway planning syndrome"
> (Harry, Care Leaver cited in Lushey and Munro, 2014, p. 15)

Likewise, there were further instances where young people felt compelled into certain courses of action in order to receive additional support. Thus drawing attention to the need for good careers advice and the correct vocational training options to be available; as Samira, revealed:

> "I ended up signing up for an HNC at college in a course I didn't really want to do as there seemed to be more support if you were going to further education. I ended up dropping out"
> (Samira, Care Leaver cited in Duncalf, 2010, p. 30)

These inconsistent approaches often meant staff had to seek resources for the young people they worked with through "begging and pleading" for services. It is clear that there does not appear to be a consistent approach by local authorities when it comes to providing services for their Care Leavers. This appears to be left to individual workers attempting to offer the best service they can within resource limits; with a culture of management reluctance to use their valuable resources without staff making themselves heard. This can often come down to the ability of the worker to articulate their wants and needs for their particular young person.

Chapter Four

4. Discussion

A discussion of the research findings is presented below; revisiting the purpose of the review in conjunction with applicative literature, theory and current social work practice in relation to young people leaving the care of the local authority. This draws together an understanding of the reliability and validity of the systematic review to assess the overall quality of the research findings. This goes hand in hand with a description of the study's limitations and the implications for future research and practice.

4.1 Revisiting the Research Aim

The aim of the review was to explore how Care Leavers aspirations compared to reality of their experiences of being in care to making the transition to independence. This was conveyed through an adherence to the voice of Care Leavers as well as those who worked alongside them.

4.2 Research Findings

Three higher order themes emerged from the study, *social isolation of Care Leavers, Care Leavers lack the skills ready for independence* and the *lack of appropriate and inconsistent approaches to the use of resources for Care Leavers*.

4.2.1 Social Isolation of Care Leavers

As a cohort group Care Leavers becoming independent are more at risk of social isolation then others by virtue of the abuse and neglect they have suffered in earlier childhood (Flemming, 1999) and that they tend to leave home at a much earlier age than their non-care peers (Stein, 2012). This is also within a period of change developmentally for adolescences as there is a shift in social relationships and experiences, such as, leaving school, going to college or seeking employment. Many seemingly face poor outcomes related to health, housing, homelessness, mental illness and unemployment (Knight, et al, 2006). These can reinforce social isolation with young people experiencing anxiety, social withdrawal and having a low perceived social efficacy (Kvarme, et al, 2010; Flood and Holmes, 2016).

The participants in the utilised studies presented their post-care experiences as something which was socially isolating. This appears to be consistent with other research findings over the decades despite young people aspiring to succeed independently (Biehal, et al, 1992; Stein and Wade, 2000; Stein, 2006b; CSJ, 2015; British Red Cross, 2016). Stein (2004; 2006b; 2010) in his work with Care Leavers suggested that weak support networks are a factor in social isolation. Being able to improve and maintain supportive relationships with others before young people leave care can improve resilience. This has been found to 'be associated with a redeeming and warm relationship with at least one person' (Stein, 2005, p. 2). In order to promote resilience consideration of the timing of when a young person leaves care is vital as this can help reduce social isolation (ibid).

The participants further suggested that social factors were high on their aspiration list for reducing social isolation and this centred on having good support from others including friends, family, professionals and having an inspirational role model. It was clear that young people wanted to share their experiences and this could be used as a form of peer education which is a highly effective way of getting messages across to young people leaving care (Whalden, 2015). This is also in line with other studies notably Selwyn and Wood (2015) who found that Care Leavers rated trusting relationships with family, friends and other adults as their main priority. Ensuring that these areas are developed is essential in reducing social isolation as the utilised studies highlight the need for young people to have someone who they can turn to.

However, Munro, et al, (2011) discovered that in some cases increasing contact with birth family led to young people being disappointed as the support on offer was not always consistent or in line with their expectations which can impact negatively on their overall well-being. In spite of this, there is still a requirement to consider family and social contacts through the pathway plan, therefore, consideration of a family group conference could promote better quality relationships. The family group conference coordinator mediates and supports a family to develop and implement their own plan with a reviewing system for success and contingency (Schmid and Pollack, 2009). Should better quality relationships and social networks develop then this will have a positive impact on reducing of social isolation.

Moreover, advocacy services, such as, Children's Rights can also support in reducing social isolation as young people have found that this 'helps them to overcome some of the barriers that exist which limit opportunities for meaningful participation and the expression of their views and interests' (Boylan and Dalrymple, 2011, p. 23). Adopting an advocacy model as described by Wilks (2012) builds on young people's existing strengths and is linked to wider support networks, leading to a greater sense of empowerment. Further to this, some local authorities have extended their Independent Visitor schemes to incorporate care leavers (Gordon and Graham, 2016). Under the *Children Act* (1989) local authorities have a duty to appoint an Independent Visitor to all Looked After children where it is in their best interests (Brammer, 2010). These volunteers befriend children and young people who suffer from social isolation. However, there is no legal duty for local authorities to promote this service to Care Leavers which can result in missed opportunities in reducing social isolation for this vulnerable cohort group.

We have also seen how the participants aspired to engage in meaningful employment or educational opportunities but barriers to that engagement prevented some from progressing which can exacerbate social isolation and exclusion (Jackson, 2007). For example, the lack of encouragement for educational attainment or funding for university accommodation. One of the best guarantees of social inclusion remains education (Jackson and Cameron, 2012). As it is widely recognised that there is a link between social isolation and lower academic attainment (Margalit, 2010). Attending college or university is a major life experience for many young people and those not in education, employment or training (NEET) has a damaging effect on them leading a happy and productive life. (Durcan and Bell, 2015). Culminating in social isolation across the life course (Marmot, 2010). Young people miss the opportunity to develop new skills and experiences which lead to greater employment opportunities which in turn effect income levels and relationships. Constrained financial circumstances and reduced support lead some Care Leavers to drop out of further and higher education (Driscoll, 2013). Greater investment and importance should be placed on services to remove the barriers which exist to create better life chances. In the long-term this will reduce the costs to the state in terms of welfare dependency (Hannon, et al, 2010).

4.2.2 Care Leavers Lack the Skills Ready for Independence

Care Leavers are not sufficiently well prepared to live independently (Brady, 2014). Some of the participants in the studies described their transition from care to independence as 'sudden' and 'rushed' and not what they thought it would be like. This is, however, conducive with other studies such as, Ward (2005); Hannon, et al, (2010); Gill and Daw (2017) and is contrary to the gradual transition to independence which is seen as most effective (Stein, 2012). The aspiration of independence is exciting for most, whereby, young people can setup home without restrictions being placed on them by carers or social workers. Nevertheless, the reality of being independent proved far more challenging for the participants.

It was clear that many failed to understand how to sustain a tenancy or pay household expenses. They lacked the necessary budgeting skills. As a consequence many found themselves in debt or on the cusp of the criminal justice system or even facing homelessness. Therefore, it is crucial that they develop good financial habits as early as possible (Ayre, et al, 2016) Yet, this has to come from staff whom support them who themselves are not always adequately trained enough to offer that support and all too often are responding to crisis management. Only taking action once a young person has reached crisis point. Care Leavers have to survive on limited income (CFW, 2017). On those grounds, managing a budget is a skill which can leave little room for savings and investment, however, they could benefit from guidance in this area in order to make long term plans.

The government recently released guidance on how to ensure young people gain independent living skills and proposed that 'encouraging young people to help with household tasks, take on weekend jobs and allowing them increasing independence will all develop important skills to make the move to independent living less daunting' (LGA, 2017, p. 9). The practicalities of allowing this to happen in an adverse risk society may prove difficult to implement pre-16 years old. Hitherto, we see an accelerated experience of leaving care between 16-18 years of age. This left many participants in the studies having to juggle multiple changes in a short period of time. It could be argued that participants missed out on part of their development which non-looked after young people experience such as gradual freedom and exploration with guided risk taking (Stein, 2005).

One of the challenges for the care system is to equip young people with the skills required for independence. Some participants received good support from their allocated workers in terms of shared learning. This helped reinforce the skills which young people learned. Taking a shared approach creates a more equal relationship akin to being *like a friend* to a young person. Previous research suggests that this way of working gives young people a more inclusive experience of engaging with services and developing new skills (McLeod, 2010).

Mentoring can also be an effective way in helping young people develop new skills (Clayden and Stein, 2005). Research suggests that young people valued the support they received participating in such schemes in relation to maintaining their accommodation, enrolling in education or seeking employment (ibid). Care Leavers share common interests which can be a powerful resource in helping each other (Thomas, 2005). Therefore an increase in peer mentoring services; especially by former care leavers can assist young people to experience a relationship which is not professional or family related (Stein, 2012). Moreover, this can be expanded into group settings and by taking a Mutual-Aid Model approach (Steinberg, 2014) individuals can benefit as well as the group as a whole. This was certainly noticed by participants who took part in the Wednesday Group.

Much of the current policy for improving outcomes for Care Leavers centres on the *Staying Put* initiative which was incorporated into legislation through the *Children and Families Act* (2014). Young people remaining in their placements post 18 will mean that they are not forced to move to independent living until they feel ready (DfE, 2013). This can allow young people to further develop their independence skills alongside a carer which in turn promotes confidence and enhances placement stability (Rock, et al, 2015).

Working with the private sector and charitable organisations can also help. For example, the National Children's Bureau developed a programme known as the Fairbridge programme (NCB, 2017) delivered by the Prince's Trust in order to help upskill Care Leavers to increase their independence levels. The programme is a week long course where Care Leavers participate in various activities and with a residential stay. There is a focus on life skills including cooking classes, curriculum vitae (C.V) writing and teambuilding exercises. Initial results appear positive with young people improving their readiness for work, have a greater commitment to achievable goals, have more impressive C.V's, increased confidence and improved peer relationships. Admittedly, there was still a significant drop out rate of a third (ibid). Further understanding is required as to why this was the case. Nonetheless, the Fairbridge programme in one example of how increasing the independence skills of Care Leavers is needed if they are going to be successful.

4.2.3 Lack of Appropriate and Inconsistent approaches to the Use of Resources for Care Leavers.

There is a lack of appropriate and inconsistent approaches taken by government and local authorities in their use of resources for Care Leavers (NCAS, 2012; Dixon and Robey, 2014; House of Commons, 2015; NAO, 2015). This was supported by many participants in the studies of their own experiences of leaving care. Unsuitable accommodation and poor quality housing were raised as concerns, with Care Leavers left in 'dingy' flats to fend for themselves. The housing charity, Centre Point (2017a) advocates for a safe and secure home as a foundation on which they can build their life after care. They see having a base as a means for them to fulfil their ambitions, gain qualifications, enter the workforce and establish themselves within the community (p. 5). This is an ideal which fails to take into account wider societal and individual factors. Social housing is in decline which means less availability and sustainability for the most in need of housing (Shelter, 2018). Many local authorities have transferred their housing stock to social landlords or have them managed by another agency such as, a tenant management organisation (TMO) (NCAS, 2009). The range of alternatives available like supported accommodation, trainer flats, foyers, supported lodgings, private sector renting and staying put with carers is limited and inconsistent between authorities. For example, only 10% of Care Leavers were living in supported accommodation (DWP & DfCLG, 2016) and there has been a low take-up of Staying Put placements (Lepper, 2015). Increasing these could enable Care Leavers to build their independent living skills with support being offered.

Further complexities exist. There is no legal requirement for local authorities to prioritise housing stock for their care leavers (Centre Point, 2017a) and priority allocations vary from area to area (Barnardo's, 2015). Young people also have to navigate the complex system of choice based lettings and bid for properties often requiring Internet access to do so which may not be available to them. Moreover, housing location impacts on Care Leavers as many can find themselves allocated homes far from familiar settings with no social networks (Action for Children, 2017). Not being aware of what to look for in a potential property can leave large numbers living in unsuitable accommodation. Care Leavers should be given the opportunity to visit and/or stay in different types of accommodation to gain first-hand experience in order to make informed decisions of where they want to live (Barnardo's, 2015). In addition, each local authority should allot a setting up home allowance for their Care Leavers. This will enable them to purchase the items they need for their new home (Short, 2002). Again, inconsistencies exist between them with regards to *need* and the sum of money allocated.

Once a Care Leaver turns 18 they can claim housing benefit through the complex Local Housing Allowance (LHA) scheme. This entitles them to the one bed LHA rate until the age of 22. When this exemption ends then the shared accommodation rate begins. This can result in a rent cliff edge as their homes become unaffordable and they have to seek alternative housing options (Children's Society, 2016; Centre Point, 2017b). Given the limited supply of social housing many young people may have to share accommodation. This could be beneficial in splitting costs and reducing social isolation but equally they could be forced to live with others they would not necessarily choose to be with.

Participant's demonstrated inconsistent approaches which local authorities took in terms of leaving care services. Some appeared to be better than others with positive praise for their workers. Leaving care forums and social groups arose out of a need for social inclusion, acceptance and learning life skills. These were often taken on by highly motivated staff who wanted the best outcomes for their young people. On the other hand there were those participants who were ambivalent towards their leaving care workers or Personal Advisors. This was mainly due to not meeting them often enough or because of high staff turnover. Similar results were found in Dixon and Robey's (2014) study suggesting frequent staff changes or never having been allocated a Personal Advisor.

This is analogous to a climate of difference in terms of caseloads which ranged from 15 to 40 which meant that some will not receive the best support and preparation for leaving care. Participants highlighted that staff spent too much time on paperwork and referred to a 'pathway planning syndrome'. This demonstrates apathy for the process with workers perhaps being too procedural. Pathways plans should be inclusive of the young person and document how their needs will be met. However, there is no consistent approach to this. Some local authorities have produced workbooks and checklists for both staff and young people as a way of assessing need and making the process more inclusive.

Additionally, the format of pathway plans differs between authorities and tends to be with what fits in for local systems (ibid); with some seeing the forms as a tick box exercise while others as the last statutory toolkit to get things right (Centre Point, 2017a). This lack of uniformity can create a gulf between good and not so good practice. Given the new *Children and Social Work Act* (2017) is due to take effect then Care Leavers will have the right to a Personal Advisor until they are 25, if they so wish. This could impact on local authorities' capacity to provide a good quality service if funding and resources are not appropriately allocated. The cost of leaving care services is expensive and varies hugely depending on area with ranges of £300 to £20,000 per Care Leaver (NAO, 2015). And a bill totalling £239 million in 2016/2017 (EFA, 2017).

The mental health costs of leaving care also come at a high price for many Care Leavers and this was highlighted throughout by participants and the professionals who worked with them. Alternative research undertaken by the Centre for Social Justice (CSJ) (2008) found that 55% of Care Leavers suffer or have suffered from depression. Child and Adolescent Mental Health Service (CAMHS) was often seen as the service which young people should be directed too. However, there was usually delays and long waiting lists for access (Mooney, et al, 2009) and a CAMHS cut off age of 18; with referral to adult mental health services where the criteria for acceptance is much higher. Some areas have developed a Youth Information Advice and Counselling Service (YIACS) which operates up to the age of 25 (DoH, 2015). This can help for continuity of care. Accessing GP services was not seen as a prominent feature for Care Leavers (Liabo, et al, 2016) but should be encouraged especially for those who attend university where there are geographical and transient locations (DoH, 2015).

Much stigma about mental health remains and young people can find it difficult to ask for help (Pugh, 2008). Services need to be flexible, accessible, taking a non-judgemental approach, if they are going to be successful. Further research by the CSJ (2011) found that staff worked better when integrated with other agencies as part of a multi-disciplinary team and this way of working should be expanded

(DoH, 2015). Where it is not possible than staff, carers and young people should have easy access to CAMHS workers for short consultations (CSJ, 2015).

4.3 Reliability and Validity of the Systematic Review

This systematic review employed an interpretive methodology to explore care leavers experiences of transition from care to independence, analysing if aspiration matched reality. This approach was purposive to the study aim exploring participants' voice in research. This was undertaken through a rigorous and systematic approach which is widely acknowledged in systematic review literature (Torgerson, 2003; Petticrew and Roberts, 2005; Gough, et al, 2012; Booth, et al, 2016). Interpretivists do not make absolute truths but look for meaning related to time, context, culture and is value bound (Mack, 2010; Manning and Kunkel, 2014). Therefore the findings presented here are based upon my own interpretations of the utilised research studies and participants experiences. Other interpretations are possible and the aim was not to seek generalizable truths for all Care Leavers. However, the findings provide a broader understanding of transition out of care.

The CASP (2017) toolkit was used to assess published research although the data was anonymised or pseudonyms used to avoid any identification. Ensuring the voice of Care Leavers remained central to the analysis was important not only to promote empowerment but to ensure developed themes remained connected to participant's own descriptions as much as possible (Larking, et al, 2006). These findings were also grounded in relevant literature, theory and current social work practice. Themes were analysed through extensive discussion with an academic supervisor and ongoing supervision provided a space for consideration of my own personal values and the potential impact on the review.

4.4 Limitations of the Systematic Review

Only one methodological approach was taken during this study. Using alternatives to re-analyse the data findings can enhance their credibility (Elliott, et al, 1999). For example the use of Grounded Theory to ascertain if there is a link between aspiration and reality may have been useful. What is more, the analysis of the results was undertaken by the author. A second analysis could yield richer findings and further increase credibility.

The study itself was active in ensuring the voice of the young people was heard, however, this is only within the limits of the ability of the participants to articulate and share experiences with the primary researcher. This could have resulted in conformity bias, whereby, participants took cues from the researcher influencing the results. (Hodges, 2017). Despite an awareness of my own personal value-base any interpretations of the research will have been influenced by personal perspectives and biases, likewise, this will be true of the participants and the primary researchers' responses to each other. Personal biases cannot be fully eliminated in qualitative research (Bryman, 2004).

4.5 Implications for Practice and Future Research

Significant practice implications materialised from the review with the data retrieved offering new insights in understanding the support needs of Care Leavers. Social Workers and Personal Advisors are the ones most involved with them and ensuring that the profession is adequately staffed, appropriately trained with proportionate caseloads and a reduction in bureaucratic processes will help mitigate against poor relationships which seem to have been the case for many. It is clear that young people value professionals who make themselves available in order to build a trusting relationship. More to the point, was the need for greater familial connections and wider social networks in order to reduce social isolation so young people can have someone to turn to when they need it the most. This will involve promoting both greater practical and emotional support such as, family group conferences, peer mentoring and independent visitor schemes. Further exploration of the reasoning behind social isolation could prove useful in enhancing the overall picture for Care Leavers.

The research also highlighted the all too often early arrival of independence for many Care Leavers before they had developed the social maturity or skills needed to live independently. Ensuring that Care Leavers are listened to is important and services should be empathetic to their needs helping them to have positive experiences of care and preventing early independence. Some of the ways to counteract this is through attachments being continued via young people remaining in placement with their carers or maintaining engagement in education, employment and the community then the situation for young people appears greatly improved.

Existing barriers need to be broken down if Care Leavers are to be successful. This will require a multi-disciplinary approach as the term *corporate parent* refers not only to the social care system but wider universal services such as, health and education (LGA, 2017b). Staff working in multiagency teams can result in better outcomes for young people as knowledge and resources can be shared (Coad, 2008). The research emphasised the need for other agencies to work more closely with social care services and allow Care Leavers who need a service to be offered this within a timely fashion.

Greater investment in leaving care services is required. The costs of not caring can be much higher in terms of monetary amounts later on in life in tackling homelessness, unemployment, mental ill-health and a life on benefits is well documented (Stein, 2005; Barnardo's, 2014). This is not to mention the human costs of allowing our Care Leavers to suffer perpetual poor outcomes.

Chapter Five

5. Conclusion

This study has sought to highlight the aspirational voice of Care Leavers as they have transitioned from care to independence and discovered if their aspirations matched the reality of their situation. There was an amalgamation of previous research undertaken through a systematic review process with an application of interpretative methodology. This allowed for overarching themes to be developed which led to an understanding of why often the aspirations of many Care Leavers were left unfulfilled.

The journey from care to independence is challenging for most Care Leavers despite having positive aspirations. This is within a period of austerity where we have seen eight years of welfare and spending cuts to public services which impact on the most vulnerable people in our society. For many Care Leavers the future for them looks very bleak with little opportunities of high salary incomes or home ownership which many aspire too. Moreover, with the spending cuts in place inevitability this leads to precious resources being ring-fenced where priority is given to one group at the expense of another.

Yet, Care Leavers remain at high risk of social exclusion where priority services are required (Pierson, 2010). This has been demonstrated through the research findings with social isolation and the lack of skills ready for independence also impacting on their future outcomes. While the resources setup to support them are often lacking or there use is inappropriately applied.

Care Leavers do require specialist services if they are going to overcome the disadvantage which they suffer. This cannot be met by universal services alone, however, this should not mean that Care Leavers are circumvented from using universal services like the rest of the population. In fact, the aim should be to provide specialist support with the intension to engage in universal services when they are ready. What is disappointing is the variation and quality of that specialist support for Care Leavers which has been highlighted throughout the research.

Moreover, both the timing and structure of when and how young people leave care is a cause for concern as this brings additional difficulties for many who simply are not ready to move on. These young people become the 'survivors' or 'strugglers' which Stein (2005) proposed. If the pathway planning process is used appropriately and creatively ensuring that young people's voices are heard and they are given the ability to exercise control in decision making the pathway plans could be much more effective.

It is important to listen and understand the experiences which Care Leavers go through as this is evidence for future social work intervention. Helping Care Leavers build safe and secure relationships with significant others is vital in combating the social isolation which many suffer from. Education provision, advocacy, mentoring and outreach work all play a central role in reducing isolation and promoting inclusion. Combined with an increase in post 18 accommodation with previous carers through schemes such as *Staying Put* or *Staying Close* and a gradual transition from care. Then this will allow Care Leavers to further develop their skills ready for independence, have easier and quicker access to support they need and better prepare them for when they are ready to be independent.

Chapter Six

6. Recommendations

Care Leavers deserve more than living in a 'dingy' flat with few opportunities and poor life chances. The following recommendations, if implemented, would help reduce social isolation, increase skills ready for independence and provide consistent and stable specialist services with a view for Care Leavers to go into adulthood when they are ready.

- Believing in Care Leavers and building on existing skills and aspirations can motivate them in their own abilities to succeed which can go a long way in helping them overcome their disadvantage in life.

- Support should be targeted and tailored to young people and be offered at a pace which they are going to engage in.

- Care Leavers should be able to make well-informed decisions about their journey to independence before those decisions are made.

- Extending time in care post 18 and ensuring that transition is gradual will improve the overall life chances for many Care Leavers.

- Promoting 'Staying Put' and 'Staying Close' arrangements to increase take-up is vital to ensure young people do not feel like they have to move on at 16 or 18.

- Social Workers and Personal Advisors should nurture the positive relationships Care Leavers have with significant others as increasing social networks will decrease social isolation which is crucial to overall well-being and allowing purposeful relationships to flourish beyond any leaving care provision.

- There should be a focus on mental health needs as well as the practical aspects of leaving care.

- Local authorities should promote role models through schemes such as, mentoring/peer mentoring, advocacy and Independent Visitor service. This can help raise self-esteem and increase aspiration.

- There needs to be a reduction in the variation of provision and an increase in joint protocols between various children's services, housing service and the Third Sector.

- Ensuring that central and local governments work together with partnership agencies to provide good quality and choice of housing for Care Leavers and the resources needed to live there.

- Care Leavers should be provided with financial and practical support to access appropriate education, employment or training which is tailored to their specific needs.

- There should be a development of work/life skills programmes nationwide for Care Leavers to prepare for independence.

- It is important that Personal Advisors are adequately trained in monetary matters in order to better support Care Leavers in their choice of financial products and services.

- Finally, maintaining a stable staff team who have positive relationships with young people can offer greater support in a time of turbulence and change for young people.

7. References

Adley, N. and Jupp Kina, V. (2017) 'Getting Behind the Closed Door of Care Leavers: Understanding the Role of Emotional Support for Young People Leaving Care', *Child and Family Social Work*, (22), pp. 97-105.

Ajetunmobi, O. (2002) *Making Sense of Critical Appraisal*. London: Hodder Arnold.

Akobeng, A. K. (2005) 'Understanding Systematic Reviews and Meta-analysis', *Archives of Disease in Childhood*, 90, pp. 845-848.

Allard, A. (2002) 'The Legislative Framework for Leaving Care'. Cited in A. Wheal, ed. (2002) *The Companion to Leaving Care*. Lyme Regis: Russell House Publishing.

Arnstein, S. (1969) 'A Ladder of Citizen Participation in the USA', *Journal of the American Institute of Planners*, 35, **(4)**, pp. 216-224.

Aveyard, H. (2010) *Doing a Literature Review in Health and Social Care: A Practical Guide*. 2nd edition. Maidenhead: McGraw-Hill.

Ayre, D., Capron, L., Egan, H., French, A. and Gregg, L. (2016) *The Cost of Being Free: The Impact of Poor Financial Education and Removal of Support on Care Leavers*. London: The Children's Society.

Baden, M. and Major, C. (20013) *Qualitative Research: The Essential Guide to Theory and Practice*. London: Routledge.

Bandura, A. (1997) *Social Learning Theory*. New York: Prentice Hill.

Barn, R., Andrew, L. and Mantovani, N. (2005) *Life After Care: The Experiences of Young People from Different Ethnic Groups*. York: Joseph Rowntree Foundation.

Barnardo's (2013) *Someone to Care: Experiences of Leaving Care*. Ilford: Barnardo's.

Barnardo's (2015) *Care Leavers Accommodation and Support Framework*. Ilford: Barnardo's

Bazelgette, L., Rahilly, T. and Trevelyan, G. (2015) *Achieving Emotional Well-being for Looked After Children: A Whole Systems Approach*. London: NSPCC.

Bentley, C. (2013) 'Great Expectations: Supporting "Unrealistic" Aspirations for Children in Care'. Cited in S. Johnson (2013) *Pathways Through Education for Young People in Care: Ideas from Research and Practice*. London: BAAF.

Berridge, D., Dance, C., Beckham, J. and Field, S. (2009) *Educating Difficult Adolescents: Effective Education for Children in Public Care or with Emotional and Behavioural Difficulties*. London: Jessica Kingsley Publishers.

Bettany-Saltikov, J. (2012) *How to do a Systematic Literature Review in Nursing: A Step-by-step Guide*. Maidenhead: McGraw Hill.

Beihal, N., Clayden, J., Stein, M. and Wade, J. (1992) *Prepared for Living? A Survey of Young People Leaving Care of Three Local Authorities*. London: National Children's Bureau.

Beylan, J. and Darlrymple, J. (2011) 'Advocacy, Social Justice and Children's Rights', *Practice: Social Work Action*, 23, **(1)**, pp. 19-30.

Booth, A., Sutton, A. and Papaioannou, D. (2016) *Systematic Approaches to a Successful Literature Review*. 2nd edition. London: Sage Publications.

Brady, R. (2014) *The Costs of Not Caring: Supporting English Care Leavers into Independence*. Ilford: Barnardo's.

Brammer, A. (2010) *Social Work Law*. 3rd edition. Harlow: Pearson Education Ltd.

Brayne, H. and Carr, H. (2010) *Law for Social Workers*. 11th edition. Oxford: Oxford University Press.

Briggs, S. (2008) *Working with Adolescents and Young Adults*. 2nd edition. Basingstoke: Palgrave Macmillan.

British Red Cross (2016) *Isolation and Loneliness: An Overview of the Literature*. London: British Red Cross.

Britzman, D. (1989) 'Who has the floor? Curriculum, Teaching and the English Student Teacher's Struggle for voice', *Curriculum Inquiry*, 19, **(2)**, pp. 143-162.

Bryman, A. (2004) *Social Research Methods*. 2nd edition. Oxford: Oxford University Press.

Burnard, P. (1991) 'A Method of Analysing Interview Transcripts in Qualitative Research', *Nurse Education Today*, 11, **(6)**, pp. 461-466.

Burls, A. (2017) 'What is Critical Appraisal?' Cited in D. Casey, L. Clark and S. Hughes (2017) *Study Skill for Master's Level Students: A Reflective Approach for Health and Social Care*. 2nd edition. Banbury: Lantern.

Cameron, R. J. and Maginn, C. (2009) *Positive Outcomes for Children in Care*. London: Sage Publications.

Cameron, C., Jackson, J., Hauari, H. and Hollingworth, K. (2012) 'Continuing Education Participation amongst Children in Care in Five Countries: Some Issues of Social Class', *Journal of Education Policy*, 27, **(3)**, pp. 387-399.

Cann, N. (2012) *The Positive Education Experiences of 'Looked After' Children and Young People*. Phd Thesis: University of East London.

Carey, M. (2009) *The Social Work Dissertation: Using Small-Scale Qualitative Methodology*. Maidenhead: McGraw Hill.

Casey, D., Clark, L. and Hughes, S. (2017) *Study Skill for Master's Level Students: A Reflective Approach for Health and Social Care*. 2nd edition. Banbury: Lantern.

Centre for Social Justice (2008) *Breakthrough Britain: Couldn't Care Less*. London: CSJ.

Centre for Social Justice (2011) *Completing the Revolution: Transforming Mental Health and Tackling Poverty*. London: CSJ.

Centre for Social Justice (2015) *Finding their Feet: Equipping Care Leavers to Reach their Potential*. London: CSJ.

Centre for Social Justice (2017) *Views from the Frontline: What do Young People Need to Move on from Care Successfully?* London: CSJ.

Centre for Reviews and Dissemination (CRD) (2008) *Systematic Reviews: CRD's Guidance for Undertaking Reviews in Health Care.* York: University of York.

Children's Rights Alliance (2016) 'United Nations has Serious Concerns about the UK Government's Failure to Prioritise Children's Needs'. Available from: http://www.crae.org.uk/newsa/united-nations-has-"serious–concerns"-about-uk-government-failure-to-prioritise-children's-needs/ [Accessed 11 November 2017].

Clayden, J. and Stein, M. (2005) *Mentoring Young People Leaving Care: Someone for Me*. York: Joseph Rowntree Foundation.

Coad, J. (2008) 'Bringing Together Child Health and Social Care Provision: Challenges and Opportunities for Multi-agency Working'. Cited in K. Morris, ed. (2008) *Social Work and Multi-agency Working: Making a Difference*. Bristol: The Policy Press.

Cocker, C. and Allain, L. (2013) *Social Work with Looked After Children*. 2nd edition. Exeter: Learning Matters.

Committee on Publication Ethics (COPE) (2017) Code of Conduct for Journal Publications. Available from https://publicationethics.org/resoucres/code-conduct [Accessed 29 December 2017].

Consumer Focus Wales (2011) *From Care to Where? How Young People Cope Financially After Care*. Cardiff: CFW.

Cossar, J., Brandon, M. and Jordan, P. (2014) 'You've Got to Trust her and she's got to Trust You: Children's Views on Participation in the Child Protection System', *Child and Family Social Work*, 21, **(1)**, pp. 103-112.

Crawford, K. and Walker, J. (2017) *Social Work and Human Development*. 5th edition. Exeter: Learning Matters.

Critical Appraisal Skills Programme (2017) *CASP Qualitative Checklist*. Available from: https://www-casp-uk.net/checklist [Accessed 08 December 2017].

Crombie, I. K. (1996) *The Pocket Guide to Critical Appraisal*. London: BMJ Publishing Group.

Davey, C. (2010) *Children's Participation in Decision-making: A Summary Report on Progress*. London: Office of Children's Commissioner and National Children's Bureau.

Department for Children, Skills and Families (2010) *Customer Voice (Wave 9): Aspirations of Children in Care*. London: DCSF.

Department for Education and Skills (2007) *Care Matters: Time for Change*. London: TSO.

Department for Education (2010) *Children Act (1989) Guidance and Regulation, Volume 3: Planning Transition to Adulthood for Care Leavers (including the Care Leavers (England) Regulations* (2010)). London: DfE.

Department for Education (2012) *Care Leaver's Charter*. London: DfE.

Department for Education (2013) *'Staying Put': Arrangements for Care Leavers age 18 and above to Stay on with their Former Foster Carers*. London: DfE.

Department for Education (2017) *Children Looked After in England including (Adoption) Year Ending 31 March 2017 Report*. London: DfE.

Department for Education & Department of Health (2015) *Promoting the Health and Wellbeing of Looked After Children: Statutory Guidance for Local Authorities, Clinical Commissioning Groups and NHS England*. London: DfE & DoH.

Department of Health (2001) *Children (Leaving Care) Act 2000: Regulations and Guidance*. London: DoH.

Department of Health (2015) *Future in Mind: Promoting, Protecting and Improving Our Children and Young People's Mental Health and Well-Being*. London: DoH.

Department for Work & Pensions and Department for Communities and Local Government (2016) *Supported Accommodation Review: The Scale, Scope and Costs of the Supported Housing Sector*. London: DWP & DfCLG.

Dixon, J., Wade, J., Byford. S., Weatherly, H. and Lee, J. (2006) *Young People Leaving Care: A Study of Costs and Outcomes. A Report to the DfES*. York: University of York.

Dixon, J. (2008) 'Young People Leaving Care: Health, Well-being and Outcomes', *Child and Family Social Work,* 13, pp. 207-217.

Dixon, L. and Robey, C. (2014) *Giving Care Leavers More Control Over their Futures: Care Leavers' Transition into Learning and Work: The Role of the Personal Advisor and the Process of Pathway Planning*. Leicester: National Institute of Adult Continuing Education (NIACE).

Driscoll, J. (2013) 'Supporting Care Leavers to Fulfil their Educational Aspirations: Resilience, Relationships and Resistance', *Children and Society*, 27, **(2)**, pp. 139-149.

Driscoll, J. (2015) 'Supporting the Education Transitions of Care Leavers: A Qualitative Investigation'. Phd Thesis: Kings College London.

Driscoll, J. (2018) *Transitions from Care to Independence: Supporting Young People Leaving Care to Fulfil their Potential*. London: Routledge.

Duncalf, Z. (2010) *Listen UP! Adult Care Leavers Speak Out: The Views of 310 Care Leavers Aged 17-78*. Manchester: Care Leavers Association.

Durcan, D. and Bell, R. (2015) *Local Action on Health Inequalities: Reducing Social Isolation Across the Life Course*. London: Public Health England.

Dwyer, S. C. and Buckle, J. L. (2009) 'The Space Between: On Being an Insider-Outsider in Qualitative Research', *Journal of Qualitative Methods*, 8, **(1)**, pp. 54-63.

Edwards, J. (2012) *'Looked After Care: Young People's Views of Making Decisions in Reviews and Planning Meetings'*, Unpublished: University of East London.

Education Funding Agency (2017) *Section 251: Budget Summary Level 2016 to 2017*. Available from: https://www.gov.uk/guidance/section-251-2016-to-2017 [Accessed 19 February 2018].

Elliott, R., Fischer, C. T. and Rennie, D. L. (1999) 'Evolving Guidelines for Publication of Qualitative Research Studies in Psychology and Related Research Fields', *British Journal of Clinical Psychology*, 39, pp. 7-10.

Ellis, M. (2002) 'Introduction to Care Leavers'. Cited in A. Wheal, ed. (2002) *The Companion to Leaving Care*. Lyme Regis: Russell House Publishing.

Fine, M. (2002) *Disrupted Voices: The Possibilities for Feminist Research*. Ann Arbour: University of Michigan Press.

Flemming, J., Mullen, P. E., Sibthorpe, B. and Bammer, G. (1999) 'The Long Term Impact of Childhood Sexual abuse in Australian Women', *Child Abuse and Neglect*, 23, **(2)**, pp. 145-159.

Flood, S. and Holmes, D. (2016) *Child Neglect and Its Relationship to Other Forms of Harm-Responding Effectively to Children's Needs: Executive Summary*. Totnes: Research in Practice (RIP), NSPCC and Action for Children.

Fraser, S., Lewis, V., Ding, S., Kellet, M. and Robinson, C., eds. (2007) *Doing Research with Children and Young People*. London: Sage Publications.

Frost, N. (2011) *Rethinking Children and Families: The Relationship Between Childhood, Families and the State*. London: Continuum International Publishing Group.

Gill, A. and Daw, E. (2017) *From Care to Where? Care Leaver's Access to Accommodation*. London: Centre Point.

Gillick vs. West Norfolk and Wisbeach Area Health Authority [1986] UK HL 7.

Goffman, E. (1963) *Stigma*. Harmondsworth: Penguin Books.

Gordon, A. and Graham, K. (2016) *The National Independent Visitor Data Report*. London: Barnardo's.

Gosall, N. and Gosall, G. (2009) *The Doctor's Guide to Critical Appraisal*. Knutsford: PasTest Ltd.

Gough, D., Oliver, S. and Thomas, J. (2012) *An Introduction to Systematic Reviews*. London: Sage Publications.

Hannon, C., Wood, C. and Bazelgette, L. (2010) *In Loco Prentis*. London: Demos.

Health and Care Professions Council (2016) *Standards of Conduct, Performance and Ethics*. London: HCPC.

Health and Care Professions Council (2017) *Standards of Proficiency: Social Workers in England*. London: HCPC.

Heath, S., Brookes, R., Cleaver, E. and Ireland, E. (2009) *Researching Young People's Lives*. London: Sage Publications.

Hiles, D., Moss, D., Thorne, L., Wright, J. and Dallos, R. (2014) 'So What Am I? Multiple Perspectives in Young People Experiences of Leaving Care', *Children and Youth Services Review*, 41, pp. 1-15.

Hill, M. (1997) 'Participatory Research with Children', *Child and Family Social Work*, 2, pp. 171-183.

H M Government (2013) *Care Leaver Strategy: A Cross-departmental Strategy for Young People Leaving Care*. London: H M Government.

Hodges, B. H. (2017) 'Conformity and Divergence in Interactions, Groups and Culture'. Cited in S. G. Harkins, K. D. Williams and J. M. Burger, eds. (2017) *Oxford Handbook of Social Influence*. Oxford: Oxford University Press.

Höjer, I. and Sjöblom, Y. (2011) 'Procedures when Young People Leave Care – Views of 111 Swedish Social Services Managers', *Children and Youth Service Review*, 33, **(12)**, pp. 2452-2460.

Holland, S. (2009) 'Listening to Children in Care: A Review of Methodological and Theoretical Approaches to Understanding Looked After Children's Perspectives', *Children and Society*, 23, pp. 226-235.

House of Commons Committee of Public Accounts (2015) *Care Leavers' Transition to Adulthood: Fifth Report of Session 2015-16*. London: The Stationary Office.

Howard League for Penal Reform (2016) 'Why do we Criminalise Young People in Care?' 6 April. Available from: http://www.russellwebber.com/criminalise-young-peopl-in-care/ [Accessed 06 March 2018].

International Federation of Social Workers/International Association of School of Social Work (2012) *Statement of Ethical Principles*. Available from: http://ifsw.org/policies/statement-of-ethical-principles/ [Accessed 11 November 2017].

Jackson, S. (2007) 'Care Leavers, Exclusions and Access to Higher Education'. Cited in D. Abrams, J. Christian and D. Gordon, eds. (2007) *Multidisciplinary Handbook of Social Exclusion Research*. New Jersey: John Wiley and Sons Ltd.

Jackson, S. and Cameron, C. (2012) 'Leaving Care: Looking Ahead and Aiming Higher', *Children and Youth Service Review*, 34, pp. 1107-1114.

Johns, R. (2017) *Using the Law in Social Work*. 7th edition. Exeter: Learning Matters.

Kellet, M., Robinson, C. and Burr, R. (2008) 'Images of Childhood'. Cited in S. Fraser, V. Lewis, S. Ding, M. Kellet and C. Robinson, eds. (2007) *Doing Research with Children and Young People*. London: Sage Publications.

Kiteley, R. and Stogdan, C. (2014) *Literature Reviews in Social Work*. London: Sage Publications.

Kirk, S. (2006) 'Methodological and Ethical Issues in Conducting Qualitative Research with Children and Young People: A Literature Review', *International Journal of Nursing Studies*, 44, pp. 1250-1260.

Kirton, D. (2007) 'The Care and Protection of Children'. Cited in J. Baldock, N. Mannay and S. Vickerstaffe, eds. (2007) *Social Policy*. 3rd edition. Oxford: Oxford University Press.

Knight, A., Chase, E. and Aggleton, P. (2006) 'Teenage Pregnancy amongst Young People in and Leaving Care: Messages and Implications for Foster Care', *Adoption and Fostering Journal*, 30, **(1)**, pp. 58-69.

Kvarme, G., Helseth, S., Sørum, R., Luth-Hansen, V., Haugland, S. and Natvig, G. K. (2010) 'The Effect of a Solution-Focused Approach to Improve Self-Efficacy in Socially Withdrawn School Children: A Non-Randomised Control Trial', *International Journal of Nursing Studies*, 47, **(11)**, pp. 1389-1396.

Larkin, M., Watts, S. and Clifton, E. (2006) 'Giving Voice and Making Sense in Interpretative Phenomenological Analysis', *Qualitative Research in Psychology*, 3, **(2)**, pp. 102-120.

Leeds Beckett University (2017) *Research Ethics Policy*. Available from: http://www.leedsbeckett.ac.uk/studenthub/research-ethics/ [Accessed 30 October 2017].

Leeson, C. (2017) 'My Life in Care: Experiences of Non-participation in Decision Making Processes', *Child and Family Social Work*, 12, **(3)**, pp. 268-277.

Legislation.gov.uk, *Children Act* (1989) Available from: http://www.legislation.gov.uk/ukpga/1989/41/ [Accessed 18 November 2017].

Legislation.gov.uk, *Children and Families Act* (2014) Available from: http://www.legislation.gov.uk/ukpga/2014/6/contents/enacted [Accessed 18 November 2017].

Legislation.gov.uk, *Children and Social Work Act* (2017) Available from: https://www.legislation.gov.uk/ukpga/2017/16/contents [Accessed 19 November 2017].

Leonard, P. (1997) 'Post Modern Welfare: Reconstruction and Emancipatory Project'. Cited in B. Humphries (2005) *Social Work Research for Social Justice*. Basingstoke: Palgrave Macmillan.

Lepper, J. (2015) 'Only a Quarter of Young People in Foster Care 'Stay Put' Past 18', *Children and Young People Now*. Available from: https://www.cypnow.co.uk/cyp/news/1153334/only-a-quarter-of-young-people-in-foster-care-'stay-put'-past-18 [Accessed 09 February 2018].

Liabo, K., McKenna, C., Ingold, A. and Roberts, H. (2016) 'Leaving Foster or Residential Care: A Participating Study of Care Leavers' Experiences of Health and Social Care Transition', *Child: Care, Health and Development*, 43, **(2)**, pp. 182-191.

Local Government Association (2017) *Support for Care Leavers: Resource Pack*. London: LGA.

Local Government Association (2009) *Provisions of Mental Health Services for Care Leavers: Transition to Adult Services*. London: LGA.

Local Government Association (2017) *Get in on the Act: Children and Social Work Act 2017*. London: LGA.

Local Government and Social Care Ombudsman (2013) *No Place Like Home: Council's Use of Unsuitable Bed and Breakfast Accommodation for Homeless Families and Young People*. Coventry: LGO.

Loughton, T. (2011) Speech to the Frank Buttle Trust Conference, gov.uk, 11 January. Available from: https://www.gov.uk/government/speeches/tim-loughton-to-the-frank-buttle-trust-conference [Accessed 19 November 2017].

Lushey, C. and Munro, E. R. (2014) 'Peer Research Methodology: An Effective Method for Obtaining Young People's Perspectives on Transition from Care to Adulthood', *Qualitative Social Work*, 14, **(4)**, pp. 522- 537.

Mack, L. (2010) 'The philosophical Underpinnings of Education Research', *Polyglossia*, 19, **(99)**, pp. 5-11.

Mahon, A., Glendinning, C., Clarke, K. and Craig, G. (1996) 'Researching Children: Methods and Ethics', *Children and Society*, 10, pp. 145-154.

Mannay, D., Staples, E., Hallett, S., Roberts, L., Rees, A., Evans, R. and Andrews, D. (2015) *Understanding the Educational Experiences and Opinions, Attainment, Achievement and Aspirations of Looked After Children in Wales: Social Research Number 62/2015*. Cardiff: Welsh Government.

Manning, J. and Kunkel, A. (2014) *Researching Interpersonal Relationships: Qualitative Methods, Studies and Analysis*. London: Sage Publications Ltd.

Marmot, M. (2010) *Fair Society, Healthy Lives: Strategic Review of Health Inequalities in England Post 2010*. London: The Marmot Review Team.

Masson J. (2007) 'The Legal Context'. Cited in S. Fraser, V. Lewis, S. Ding, M. Kellet and C. Robinson, eds. (2007) *Doing Research with Children and Young People*. London: Sage Publications.

McDonald, P., Pini, B., Bailey, J. and Price, R. (2011) 'Young People's Aspirations for Education, Work, Family and Leisure', *Work, Employment and Society*, 25, **(1)**, pp. 68-84.

McLaughlin, H. (2007) *Understanding Social Work Research*. London: Sage Publications.

McLeod, A. (2010) 'A Friend and Equal: Do Young People in Care Seek the Impossible from their Social Workers', *British Journal of Social Work*, 40, **(3)**, pp. 772-788.

Meline, T. (2006) 'Selecting Studies for Systematic Reviews: Inclusion and Exclusion Criteria', *Contemporary Issues in Communication Science and Disorders*, 33, pp. 21-27.

Miles, M. and Huberman, A. (1994) *Qualitative Data Analysis: An Expanded Sourcebook*. London: Sage Publications.

Mooney, M., Stratham, J., Monck, M. and Chambers, H. (2009) 'Promoting the Health of Looked After Children: A Study to Inform Revision of the 2002 Guidelines', *Research Report*. London: DCSF.

Morgan, R. (2012) *After Care: Young People's Views of Leaving Care: Reported by the Children's Rights Director for England*. London: Ofsted.

Morse, J. M., Barrett, M., Mayan, M., Olson, K. and Spiers, J. (2002) 'Verification Strategies for Establishing Reliability and Validity in Qualitative Research', *International Journal of Qualitative Methods*, 1, **(2)**, pp. 13-22.

Munro, E., Lushey, C., Ward, H. and National Care Advisory Service (NCAS) (2011) *Evaluation of the Right2BCared4 Pilots: Final Report*. London: DfE.

National Association for Care and Resettlement of Offenders (2012) *Reducing Offending by Looked After Children*. London: NACRO.

National Audit Office (2015) *Care Leavers' Transition to Adulthood*. London: NAO

National Audit Office (2016) *Children and Young People in Care and Leaving Care*. London. NAO.

National Care Advisory Service (NCAS) (2009) *Journeys to Home: Care Leavers' Successful Transition to Independent Accommodation*. London: DfCF.

National Care Advisory Service (NCAS) (2012) *Access All Areas: Action for All Government Departments to Support Young People's Journey from Care to Adulthood*. London: Catch 22.

National Children's Bureau (2017) *Research Summary: From Care to Independence*. London: NCB.

National Society for the Prevention of Cruelty to Children (2014) *Promoting the Wellbeing of Children in Care: Messages from Research*. London: NCPCC.

Nerey, M. (2016) *Residential Care in England: Report of Sir Martin Nerey's Independent Review of Children's Residential Care*. London DfE.

Office for Standards in Education, Children's Services and Skills (2009) *Support for Care Leavers*. London: Ofsted.

Okolosie, L. (2015) 'What Chance do Care Leavers Stand with Support Services being Shredded?' *The Guardian Newspaper,* 16 December. Available from: https://www.theguardian.com/commentisfree/2015/dec/16/care-leavers-support-services-mental-health [Accessed 19 November 2017].

O'Loughlin, M. and O'Loughlin, S. (2012) *Social Work with Children and Families*. 3rd edition. Exeter: Learning Matters.

Oxford English Dictionary (2017) Available from: https://www.oed.com [Accessed 18 November 2017].

Parton, N. and Kirk, S. (2010) 'The Nature and Purpose of Social Work'. Cited in I. Shaw, K. Briar-Lawson, J. Orm and R. Ruckdeschel, eds. (2010) *The Sage Handbook of Social Work Research*. Los Angles: Sage Publications.

Pierson, J. (2010) *Tackling Social Exclusion*. 2nd edition. London: Routledge.

Petticrew, M. and Roberts, H. (2005) *Systematic Reviews in the Social Sciences: A Practical Guide*. Oxford: Blackwell Publishing.

Pond, S. (2011) 'Social Work and Social Workers Power: A Lay Perspective'. Cited in T. Okitikpi, ed. (2011) *Social Control and the Use of Power in Social Work with Children and Families*. Lyme Regis: Russell House Publishing.

Pugh, K. (2008) 'Stressed Out and Struggling: Making the Transition from Child to Adult'. Cited in C. Jackson, K. Hill and P. Lavis, eds. (2008) *Child and Adolescent Mental Health Today: A Handbook*. Brighton: Pavilion Publishing Ltd.

Pycroft, A., Wallis, A., Bigg, J. and Webster, G. (2015) 'Participation, Engagement and Change: A Study of the Experiences of Service Users of the Unified Adolescent Team', *British Journal of Social Work*, 45, pp. 422-439.

Race, T. and O'Keefe, R. (2017) *Child-Centred Practice: A Handbook for Social Work*. London: Palgrave Macmillan.

Reed in Partnership Ltd (2011) *From Care to Independence: Improving Employment Outcomes for Care Leavers*. London: Reed Ltd.

Rees, A., Beecroft, C. and Booth, A. (2010) 'Critical Appraisal of the Evidence'. Cited in K. Gerrish and A. Lacey, eds. (2010) *The Research Process in Nursing*. 6th edition. Oxford: Blackwell Publishing.

Robson, C. (2002) *Real World Research*. 2nd edition. Oxford: Blackwell Publishing.

Sinclair, R. and Franklin, A. (2000) *Young People's Participation: Quality Protects Research Briefing, No. 3*. London: DoH.

Rock, S., Michelson, D., Thomson, S. and Day, C. (2015) 'Understanding Foster Placement Instability for Looked After Children: A Systematic Review and Narrative Synthesis of Quantitative and Qualitative Evidence', *British Journal of Social Work*, 45, **(1)**, pp.177-203.

Schmid, J. E. and Pollack, S. (2009) 'Developing Shared Knowledge: Family Group Conferencing as a Norm of Negotiating Power in the Child Welfare System', *Practice: Social Work Action*, 21, **(3)**, pp. 175-188.

Selwyn, J. and Wood, M. (2015) *Children and Young People's Views on Being in Care: A Literature Review*. Hadley Centre for Adoption and Foster Care Studies, Coram Voice. Bristol: University of Bristol.

Sheldon, B. and MacDonald, G. (2009) *A Text-book of Social Work*. Oxon: Routledge.

Shelter (2018) 'Why We Need More Social Housing'. Available from: http://england.shelter.org.uk/campaigns_/why_we_campaign/Improving_social_housing/Why_we_need_more_social_housing [Accessed 09 February 2018].

Shenton, A. K. (2004) 'Strategies for Ensuring Trustworthiness in Qualitative Research Projects', *Education for Information*, 22, pp. 63-77.

Short, J. (2002) 'Financial Arrangements for Care Leavers: Developing a Service'. Cited in A. Wheal, ed. (2002) *The Companion to Leaving Care*. Lyme Regis: Russell House Publishing Ltd.

Slee, K. (2016) 'Young Care Leavers Need More than Just a Home to Avoid Homelessness', The Guardian Newspaper, 30 August. Available from: https://www.theguardian.com/housing-network/2016/aug/30/young-care-leaver-homelessnesss-support-independant [Accessed 12 November 2017].

Smith, N. (2107) *Neglected Minds: A Report on Mental Health Support for Young People Leaving Care*. London. Barnardo's.

Smith, W. B. (2011) *Youth Leaving Foster Care: A Developmental, Relationship-based Approach to Practice*. Oxford: Oxford University Press.

Social Care Institute for Excellence (2012) Research Mindedness: Critical Appraisal. Available from: https://www.scie.org.uk/publications/researchmindedness/findingresources/assessingresearchquality/ [Accessed 12 November 2017].

Social Exclusion Unit (2003) *A Better Education for Children in Care*. London: HMSO.

Spittlehouse, C., Acton, M. and Enock, K. (2000) 'Introducing Critical Appraisal Skills Training in UK Social Services: Another Link Between Health and Social Care', *Journal of Interprofessional Care*, 14, **(4)**, pp. 397-404.

Stein, M. (2004) *What Works for Young People Leaving Care?* Ilford: Barnardo's.

Stein, M. (2005) *Resilience and Young People Leaving Care: Overcoming the Odds*. York: Joseph Rowntree Foundation.

Stein, M. (2006a) 'Research Review: Young People Leaving Care', *Child and Family Social Work,* 11, pp. 273-279.

Stein, M. (2006b) 'Young People Aging Out of Care: The Poverty of Theory', *Children and Youth Service Review*, (28), pp. 422-434.

Stein, M. (2009) *Quality Matters in Children's Services: Messages from Research*. London: Jessica.

Stein, M. (2010) 'Transitions from Care to Adulthood: Messages from Research for Policy and Practice'. Cited in M. Stein and E. R. Munro, eds. (2010) *Young People's Transition from Care to Adulthood: International Research and Practice*. London: Jessica Kinsley Publishers.

Stein, M. (2012) *Young People Leaving Care: Supporting Pathways to Adulthood*. London: Jessica Kingsley Publishers.

Stein, M. and Wade, J. (2000) *Helping Care Leavers: Problems and Strategic Responses*. London: DoH.

Steinberg, D. M. (2014) *A Mutal-Aid Model for Social Work with Groups*. 3rd edition. London and New York: Routledge.

Thomas, N. (2005) *Social Work with Young People in Care: Looking After Children in Theory and Practice*. Basingstoke: Palgrave Macmillan.

Torgerson, C. (2003) *Systematic Reviews*. London: Continuum International Publishing Group.

Unicef (2004) *The United Nations Conventions of the Rights of Child*. London: Unicef UK.

United Nations Committee on the Rights of the Child (2016-d) *Concluding Observation of the Fifth Periodic Report of the United Kingdom of Great Britain and Northern Ireland CRC/C/GBR/CO/5*. Geneva: Office of the United Nations High Commissioner for Human Rights (OHCHR).

Universities UK (2012) *The Concordat to Support Research Integrity*. London: Universities UK.

Wade, J. (2008) 'The Ties that Bind: Support from Birth Families and Substitute Families for Young People Leaving Care', *British Journal of Social Work*, (38), pp. 39-54.

Waterhouse, R. (2000) *Lost in Care: Summary of Report*. London: Stationary Office.

Wilks, T. (2012) *Advocacy and Social Work Practice*. Maidenhead: Open University Press.

Winter, K. (2006) 'The Participation Rights of Looked After Children in Health Care: A Critical Review of the Research', *The International Journal of Children's Rights*, 14, pp. 77-95.

Whalen, A. (2015) *Provision for Young Care Leavers at Risk of Homelessness*. Wales: Public Policy Institute for Wales.

Appendix A.

Table of Utilised Studies

No.	Author	Aim	Sample	Method	Results	Discussion
1	Dixon J. (2008)	To explore the outcomes and service costs focussing on health and well-being of young people making the transition from care to independent adulthood	106 young people who had left care in seven local authorities	Based upon previous research carried out by the author with qualitative face-to-face interviews conducted 3 months of leaving care focusing on care careers, preparation for adulthood and initial post-care outcomes as a base-line. Parallel telephone interviews with leaving care workers with triangulation of data reported. Follow-up interviews at 12 months with 101 young people taking part which explored the progress they had made in key life events. The General Health Questionnaire	Evidence of need related to physical and mental health on care leavers during their transition from care to independence. Evidence of poor mental health such as depression, anxiety and substance misuse. From baseline to follow-up mental health problems increased such as stress and anxiety with 4 young people attempting suicide; which could be linked to the actual process of transitioning from care to independence. Evidence of clear housing instability, homelessness, unemployment and living on limited resources. Moving to independent living at an early age and encountering a number of key transitional stages had impact.	The transition from care raises new challenges; earlier pre- and in-care experiences can affect a young person's overall health and well-being. With further links demonstrated on their lives in progression of finding a home and embarking upon a career. There appears to be a need for greater effective preparation for independent living and easier, flexible access to after care support services. Ensuring young people have opportunities to develop a sense of achievement are important ingredients in enabling them to reach their full potential and overall well-being. A more collaborative approach with health services was emerging, however, a

				(GHQ-12) was administered at baseline and follow-up to assess change in mental health and general well-being overtime. Data analysis was based upon existing theory and identified themes.	Realities and difficulties of post-care living could trigger past emotional experiences and impact on coping strategies.	more co-ordinated, well-resourced and wide-ranging health strategy is required.
2	Dunclaf, Z. (2010)	To report and describe the voices of Care Leavers and their experiences of being in care and of leaving care	310 Care Leavers aged between 17-78	A mixed-method approach via an on-line questionnaire developed by the Care Leavers Association (CLA) which aimed to gather information relating to the experiences of being in care and leaving care. A small on-line pilot study was carried out prior to the main study going live. An on-line link was provided on the CLA website and	Evidence of disability occurring in or after care as a result of care experiences such as, Post-Traumatic Stress Disorder (PTSD) or agoraphobia. A raise of importance of sexual orientation and ethnicity as problematic and affected by experiences of being in care. A greater understanding of what it meant to be a young persons in care where there was a lack of understanding and connection with others. Lack of support, poor accommodation/hom	Care Leavers face a variety of difficulties that can derive from their in-care experiences and from leaving care often struggling with them throughout their lives. It should not be assumed that younger care leavers have more positive outcomes upon leaving care or that it has radically changed over time. There needs to be greater involvement of care leavers in research, policy and practice. However, there is a feeling of frustration that this is not an option open to them.

				mass emails to all the networks available to the CLA including 5,000 people registered on the website 'Care Leavers Reunited.com'. The study was also advertised in the CLA newsletter with Care Leavers being encouraged to share this with other care leavers. Descriptive analysis of the qualitative data was used.	elessness, isolation/abandonment, financial difficulties, lack of employment opportunities were identified as main themes for care leavers as they made their transition from care to independence.	
3	Barnardo's (2013)	To understand more about the most vulnerable Care Leavers and the support provided to offer them the best help with making the	62 young people	In-depth qualitative interviews and focus groups with care leavers and workers supporting them with descriptive analysis of the challenges faced by care leavers as they make their transition to adult life.	Pre-care experiences raised as an issue for care leavers. Evidence of multiple moves of placements and of changes of social workers resulting in no constant adult to rely on growing up and nowhere to call home. Raising feelings of 'sudden' and 'raw' on leaving care and 'tough and 'lonely' once living alone	Local authorities and supporting agencies need to continue to prepare care leavers to enter adult life, offering advice, care and guidance. Longer periods of support will offer greater opportunities to them and there is a need for all young people leaving care to 'stay put' in their placements until they are 21.

		transition to adulthood			with mental health being a concern. Homelessness, unsuitable accommodation and risk of eviction raised as an issue. The need to remain in placement longer; post 18. Budgeting and debt seen as a serious source of anxiety for care leavers with a reliance on welfare benefits. Community participation has a stabilising effect.	
4	Hiles, D., Moss, D., Thorne, L., Wright, J. and Dallos, R. (2014)	To seek to give a voice to young people and the professionals working alongside them, in their transition from care. Aiming to surface their experiences of	6 White British male Care Leavers aged between 16-22. 4 Health & Social Care Professionals – 3 female and 1	A pilot study which employed a cross-sectional qualitative design based on action research to obtain data from two focus groups. One with care leavers the other with professionals. Ethnographical and auto-ethnographical data analysis employed alongside separate	Three core themes identified from care leavers; *leaving the system*, *the constantly changing social network* and *the lived experience of support*. These were broken down further into sub-themes. Three core themes identified from professionals; *the train wreck at 18*, *service design and development* and *working as a professional*. Again, broken down into sub-themes.	Care Leavers main preoccupation appears to be trying to make the transition to independence work while developing a new identity in the midst of an unstable environment. Independence was seen as a goal which could be inappropriate and forced upon them resulting in poor outcomes and the experience of powerlessness. Staff turnover and caseload pressures

		this transition and support available	male	thematic analysis to identify key themes. The focus groups were transcribed and loaded into NVivo 10 for coding. Further validity enhancement techniques used in some areas in terms of journal recording and memory checking. A triangulation approach adopted.		resulted in individual variability of support.
5	Lushey, C. and Munro, E. R. (2014)	To explore the advancement of participatory peer research methodology in research with children in and leaving care as they make their	28 Care Leaver peer researchers	Peer research methodology employed. A job description developed and distributed to participating local authorities who in most cases identified participants. 28 peer researchers recruited, however, 7 remained involved until completion. Three training	Evidence of staff placing an emphasis on the bureaucratic process of completing paperwork at the expense of spending time with young people. Importance of carers maintaining contact with former Looked After children, after care. There appeared to be missed opportunities to probe further from peer researchers due to the lack of	The importance of eliciting young people's views to improve policy and practice to meet need. Peer research methodology serves to empower young people to participate in research by reducing power imbalances and bias to allow children and young people's voices to be heard.

| | | transition from care to independence | | events held for peer researchers. Face-to-face interviews undertaken by peer researches with research participants. Peer researchers actively involved in the thematic analysis of the qualitative data through coding transcripts and identifying key findings. | experience and limited training. | |

Appendix B.

Critical Appraisal Skills Programme (CASP) Qualitative Checklist

10 questions to help you make sense of qualitative research

How to use this appraisal tool

Three broad issues need to be considered when appraising a qualitative study:

Are the results of the study valid?   (Section A)
What are the results?   (Section B)
Will the results help locally?   (Section C)

The 10 questions on the following pages are designed to help you think about these issues systematically. The first two questions are screening questions and can be answered quickly. If the answer to both is "yes", it is worth proceeding with the remaining questions.

There is some degree of overlap between the questions, you are asked to record a "yes", "no" or "can't tell" to most of the questions. A number of italicised prompts are given after each question. These are designed to remind you why the question is important. Record your reasons for your answers in the spaces provided.

These checklists were designed to be used as educational pedagogic tools, as part of a workshop setting, therefore we do not suggest a scoring system. The core CASP checklists (randomised controlled trial & systematic review) were based on JAMA 'Users' guides to the medical literature 1994 (adapted from Guyatt GH, Sackett DL, and Cook DJ), and piloted with health care practitioners.

For each new checklist a group of experts were assembled to develop and pilot the checklist and the workshop format with which it would be used. Over the years overall adjustments have been made to the format, but a recent survey of checklist users reiterated that the basic format continues to be useful and appropriate.

Referencing: we recommend using the Harvard style citation, i.e.:

Critical Appraisal Skills Programme (2017). CASP (insert name of checklist i.e. Qualitative Research) Checklist. [online] Available at: *URL*. Accessed: *Date Accessed*.

©CASP this work is licensed under the Creative Commons Attribution – Non Commercial-Share A like. To view a copy of this license, visit http://creativecommons.org/licenses/by-nc-sa/3.0/ www.casp-uk.net

Screening Questions

1. Was there a clear statement of the aims of the research? ☐ Yes ☐ Can't tell ☐ No

HINT: Consider
- What was the goal of the research?
- Why it was thought important?
- Its relevance

2. Is a qualitative methodology appropriate? ☐ Yes ☐ Can't tell ☐ No

HINT: Consider
- If the research seeks to interpret or illuminate the actions and/or subjective experiences of research participants
- Is qualitative research the right methodology for addressing the research goal?

Is it worth continuing?

Detailed questions

3. Was the research design appropriate to address the aims of the research? ☐ Yes ☐ Can't tell ☐ No

HINT: Consider
- If the researcher has justified the research design (E.g. have they discussed how they decided which method to use)?

©Critical Appraisal Skills Programme (CASP) Qualitative Research Checklist 13.03.17

4. Was the recruitment strategy appropriate to the aims of the research? ☐ Yes ☐ Can't tell ☐ No

HINT: Consider
- If the researcher has explained how the participants were selected
- If they explained why the participants they selected were the most appropriate to provide access to the type of knowledge sought by the study
- If there are any discussions around recruitment (e.g. why some people chose not to take part)

---

5. Was the data collected in a way that addressed the research issue? ☐ Yes ☐ Can't tell ☐ No

HINT: Consider
- If the setting for data collection was justified
- If it is clear how data were collected (e.g. focus group, semi-structured interview etc.)
- If the researcher has justified the methods chosen
- If the researcher has made the methods explicit (e.g. for interview method, is there an indication of how interviews were conducted, or did they use a topic guide)?
- If methods were modified during the study. If so, has the researcher explained how and why?
- If the form of data is clear (e.g. tape recordings, video material, notes etc)
- If the researcher has discussed saturation of data

---

6. Has the relationship between researcher and participants been adequately considered? ☐ Yes ☐ Can't tell ☐ No

HINT: Consider
- If the researcher critically examined their own role, potential bias and influence during
  (a) Formulation of the research questions
  (b) Data collection, including sample recruitment and choice of location
- How the researcher responded to events during the study and whether they considered the implications of any changes in the research design

©Critical Appraisal Skills Programme (CASP) Qualitative Research Checklist 13.03.17

7. Have ethical issues been taken into consideration? ☐ Yes ☐ Can't tell ☐ No

HINT: Consider
- If there are sufficient details of how the research was explained to participants for the reader to assess whether ethical standards were maintained
- If the researcher has discussed issues raised by the study (e.g. issues around informed consent or confidentiality or how they have handled the effects of the study on the participants during and after the study)
- If approval has been sought from the ethics committee

---

8. Was the data analysis sufficiently rigorous? ☐ Yes ☐ Can't tell ☐ No

HINT: Consider
- If there is an in-depth description of the analysis process
- If thematic analysis is used. If so, is it clear how the categories/themes were derived from the data?
- Whether the researcher explains how the data presented were selected from the original sample to demonstrate the analysis process
- If sufficient data are presented to support the findings
- To what extent contradictory data are taken into account
- Whether the researcher critically examined their own role, potential bias and influence during analysis and selection of data for presentation

---

©Critical Appraisal Skills Programme (CASP) Qualitative Research Checklist 13.03.17

9. Is there a clear statement of findings? ☐ Yes ☐ Can't tell ☐ No

HINT: Consider

- If the findings are explicit
- If there is adequate discussion of the evidence both for and against the researchers arguments
- If the researcher has discussed the credibility of their findings (e.g. triangulation, respondent validation, more than one analyst)
- If the findings are discussed in relation to the original research question

10. How valuable is the research?

HINT: Consider

- If the researcher discusses the contribution the study makes to existing knowledge or understanding e.g. do they consider the findings in relation to current practice or policy?, or relevant research-based literature?
- If they identify new areas where research is necessary
- If the researchers have discussed whether or how the findings can be transferred to other populations or considered other ways the research may be used

Appendix C.

Examples of Extracted and Synthesised Data Leading to Sub-themes and Higher Order Themes

	Colour-coded criteria	Data Extracted	Sub-themes	Higher Order Themes
Aspirational voice of the Care Leaver	Red	(you want) "someone being there for you" – Care Leaver. "To be given a chance" (for a job) – Care Leaver. "The best help would be for someone to talk to… I would love that" – Care Leaver. "I'd rather be back in care" – Care Leaver. "To be given the help to 'come out' ended up being a positive experience" – Care Leaver "To have a role model and not be a burden to everyone" – Care Leaver. "They should come out of care with a skill to trade to equip them to enter the world of work" – Care Leaver "my worker, he just gets you up, just like that. He just really got my confidence" – Care Leaver "There should be a preparation course prior to leaving care on everyday living, relationships, budgeting, self-esteem and the like" – Care Leaver. "A university grant of 33 weeks and I had to make it last 52 weeks… I was unable to live in Halls and I had to find accommodation that wasn't going to turf me out during the	Advocacy Social isolation Emotional and social support Role modelling Powerlessness Independent living skills Accommodation and support issues Educational attainment	Social isolation of Care Leavers

		holidays" – Care Leaver "I wanted to go to college when I left school but was told I had to get a job and move out" – Care Leaver. "People have different social networks for doing different things, like some people obviously will have their friends who will go out drinking with them because all do the same thing and they'll have a laugh together…and then they'll have, like another group of friends, like, where they maybe go to college together"		
Reality of being independent	Blue	"I suppose you get different people for different support depending on what relationship you have with them, cause you'll go to somebody for help finding a job (or) wanting a CV" – Care Leaver. 'Post Care living could trigger or intensify past emotional issues which in turn affect health and coping strategies' – Researcher reflection. "I have just been a bit lonely and down… since I've had this flat I've had lots of time on my own thinking more about not being with anyone and missing things" – Care Leaver. "I haven't spoken to (my old foster carer) for about a year" – Care Leaver. "If I had parents to go to, I would go to my parents and ask for their help. Or I'd stay with my parents so the strain wouldn't be	Too many adults involved no one person to rely on Mental ill-health Social isolation Aging out of care with the necessary skills Lack of opportunity and sense of achievement Low self-	

		so much. But I don't have anybody. I don't have anyone to turn to" – Care Leaver.	esteem	Care Leavers lack the skills ready for independence
		"Once you're 16, you move out of your foster home and then semi-independent. And then you're 18, leaving care. The day of your 18th birthday, they will kick you out" – Care Leaver.	Financial resource limitation	
			Social and emotional difficulties	
		"I was too young at 16" (to live independently) – Care Leaver	Homelessness and unemployment	
		"I was suffering really bad with depression and… I was so down" (when in my own accommodation) – Care Leaver.		
		"If I am alone to long I self-harm and think about suicide and stuff. I try to keep my day and night busy 24/7. It is hard but I get by – Care Leaver living independently.		
		"I couldn't cope… I didn't know how to pay bills. I didn't know what letters meant when they came through the post" – Care Leaver.		
		"When I am at home I try to use little (gas) as possible. But the electricity I don't know how much I'm using" – Care Leaver.		
		"I was not disabled when I was in care but due to my in-care experiences I have agoraphobia and social difficulties which have led to serious mental health problems which I think are a product of being in care" – Care Leaver.		
		"Not nice, I was homeless, unemployed, very hungry, very lonely, and scared of the future and the present. I did not even know how to sign on to get money and ended up		

		shop lifting" – Care Leaver. "Yeah, I hated living on my own. I couldn't cope at first…I didn't know how to pay bills or council tax. I didn't know what the letters meant when they came through the post" – Care Leaver		
The system currently in place to support Care Leavers	Green	"Forced or pointless support" (being offered) – Care Leaver. "Social Services are modelling the client… we are responding to chaos and reaction to crises" – Professional. There's "begging and pleading (for services to prevent) "the train-wreck at 18" – Professional. "He won't accept the support he needs" – Professional. (staff) "spend too much time on paperwork we call it the pathway planning syndrome" – Care Leaver. "We setup the Wednesday evening (group) and they got benefit from just coming and having a chat and interacting with each other. We do cook-and-eat" – Professional. "I ended up signing up for an HNC at college in a course I didn't really want to do as there seemed to be more support if you were going to further education. I ended up dropping out" – Care Leaver. "It's like a train wreck…yes, it's like a train wreck, suddenly at 18. I definitely articulate	Forced support or inappropriate support High levels of bureaucracy Community participation helpful Lack of	Lack of appropriate resources for Care Leavers

		"that to young people as best I can and say you might be kicking against us right now but at 18 it will be most likely quite a different world" – Professional.	integrated services	
		"I was always called a Care Leaver from the age of 16 upwards anyway, so it was like, so what I am? I'm a Care Leaver all between 16 and 21 but I'm still in care, so how come I'm a Care Leaver" – Care Leaver.	Inconsistent approaches to service delivery	
		"Poor housing can affect a young person's health and in turn damage their coping strategies" – Researcher Reflection.		
		"locally CAMHS is very restrictive…there isn't anything local that is tailor made for young people" – Professional.	High caseloads	
		"Poor housing situations, being unemployed and lacking supporting networks had allowed [a young person] to dwell on childhood experiences" – Researcher Reflection.	Lack of suitable accommodation	
		"my main issue is of what I am going through right now, I have left the care system this year in January. I rang up my social worker to talk and she said she wasn't on the team anymore. She gave me another number for the team in [Somewhere else]. I spoke to another lady who said she was my new care leaver worker and that we should meet up for a coffee. It's August. Enough said I think. The point I am trying to make is yes we are adults, but we still need help!" – Care Leaver.		
		"adult support comes from often selected support workers with caseload ranging		

between 15 and 40 young people" – Research Reflection.

"I'm Ellie's…worker but she's teaching me the culinary skills, because you're such a good cook, aren't you? You showed me how to make soup, last week. So it's about learning from each other as well. Even though we're staff, we learn from the young people, it's about working together as a team" – Professional.

"Housing instability, homelessness, unemployment and living on limited financial resources…after leaving care, all of which could impact on general health" – Researcher Reflection.

"We are the people who counselled him and we're not equipped in that department" – Professional.

9. Index

A

Abuse   3, 11, 42
Action research   25, 26, 78
Adolescent   4, 13, 49
Adoption   3
Adulthood   1, 14, 22, 34, 55, 75, 78
Advice   4, 40, 49, 77
Advocacy   43, 54, 56, 88
Aimhigher programme   7
Ambition   7, 47
Analysis   ii, 17, 20, 21, 22, 25, 26, 27, 29, 50, 76, 77, 78, 79, 80
Anonymity   25, 28
Anxiety   30, 42, 75, 78
Appraisal (see CASP)
Apprenticeships   36
Aspirations   ii, 1, 7, 8, 9, 12, 13, 14, 16, 17, 19, 53, 55
Assessment   5, 14, 21, 22, 25
Attachment   9, 10, 52

B

Barnardo's   7, 14, 19, 23, 24, 25, 26, 30, 31, 32, 33, 34, 36, 38, 39, 47, 48, 52, 77
Befriend   5, 43
Benefits   52, 78
Bias   1, 24, 51, 79
Birthday   1, 13, 31, 34, 38, 90
Boolean logic   16, 1
Brammer, A.   3, 5, 6, 43
Budgeting   35, 44, 78, 88

C

Care
  being in   ii, 1, 9, 14, 41, 76, 90
  experiencing   9
  leaving   1, 2, 3, 4, 5, 9, 16, 31, 34, 35, 37, 42 45, 47, 48, 49, 55, 75, 76, 77, 79, 88, 90
  substitute   4
  system   1, 2, 6, 7, 34, 38, 40, 45, 52, 92
Care Leaver Charter   12
Care Leavers (England Regulations) (2010)   5
Care Order   2
Care plan   3
Care settings
  children's homes   3, 38
  independent living   ii, 1, 3, 34, 45, 47, 75
  placement with parents   3
  secure unit   3
  semi-independent living   3, 34
Career   8, 9, 39, 40, 75
Child and Adolescent Mental Health (CAMHS)   13, 38, 49, 50, 92
Childhood   4, 9, 11, 37, 42, 92
Children Act (1989)   2, 3, 11, 43
Children (Leaving Care) Act (2000)   4, 5
Children & Families Act (2014)   8, 13, 46
Children & Social Work Act (2017) 4, 5, 14, 49
Children's Rights   11, 43
Confidentiality   vi, 28
Contact   2, 3, 5, 32, 43, 79
Consent   12, 26
Community   1, 39, 47, 52, 78, 91
Corporate parent   2, 52
'Criminalise'   6
Criminal Justice System   1, 13, 32, 45
Critical Appraisal Skills Toolkit (CASP)   21, 81
Curriculum Vitae (C.V)   46

D

Database   15, 16, 17
Data collection   24
Department for Education   3, 16
Depression   30, 49, 75, 90
'Devaluation'   6
Discrimination v, 6, 7
Dixon, J.   19, 23, 34, 25, 26, 30, 37, 38, 40, 47, 48, 75
Driscoll, J.   6, 7, 8, 9, 10, 13, 44
Duncalf, Z.   2, 19, 23, 24, 25, 26, 30, 31, 32, 33, 34, 35, 36, 39, 40

E

Education   1, 3, 4, 5, 7, 8, 9, 10, 13, 16, 33, 36, 40, 42, 44, 45, 52, 54, 56, 88, 91
  accreditation   35
  attainment   1, 7, 9, 44
  college   2, 32, 33, 40, 42, 44, 89, 91
  further   36, 40, 91
  higher   7, 44
  university   9, 15, 21, 25, 26, 27, 28, 33, 44, 49, 88
Eligible child   4
Employment   1, 4, 8, 13, 33, 42, 43, 44, 45, 52, 56, 77
Empower & empowerment   7, 11, 24, 43, 50, 79
Ethics & ethical issues   6, 25, 26, 27, 28

F

Family   iii, 3, 4, 8, 9, 10, 42, 43, 46
Family Group Conference   43, 52
Financial issues   8, 13, 33, 37, 44, 45, 56, 77, 93
Former Relevant   4
Forums   38, 49
Foster carer   32, 89
Frost, N.   6, 28

G

GCSE's   9
Gillick Competence   12
Google & *google* scholar   15, 16, 17, 18
Government   12, 13, 14, 16, 20, 26, 45, 47, 56
Grey literature   15, 17
Grounded theory   50, 51

H

Health   4, 7, 10, 13, 14, 17, 19, 21, 28, 30, 37, 38, 39, 49, 52, 56, 75, 76, 78, 89, 90, 92
Health & Care Professions Council   vi, 27
Homelessness   4, 10, 19, 37, 42, 45, 52, 76, 78, 90, 93
Housing   1, 13, 37, 38, 39, 42, 48, 56, 75, 92, 93
Howard League of Penal Reform   6

I

Income   33, 44, 45, 53
Identity   vi, 4, 6, 10, 12, 25, 28, 35, 78
Independence   ii, 4, 5, 6, 7, 8 ,9, 10, 14, 15, 16, 17, 19, 22, 23, 29, 31, 33, 34, 35, 36, 41, 44, 45, 46, 50, 52, 53, 54, 55, 56, 75, 77, 78, 80, 90
Independent Visitor   43, 52, 56
Integrity   vi, 27
Interpretivist   20, 29, 50
Isolation (isolated)   ii, 1, 10, 29, 30, 31, 32, 33, 41, 42, 43, 44, 48, 51, 52, 53, 54, 55, 77, 88, 89

L

Ladder of participation   11
Leaving home   1
Leisure   33
Life chances   ii, 1, 6, 10, 44, 55
Life course   44
Limitations   21, 41, 51

Local authorities   2, 5, 12, 13, 35, 40, 43, 47, 48, 49, 56, 75, 77, 79
Loci parentis   2
Lonely   10, 29, 30, 31, 77, 89, 90
Looked After Children   1, 3, 6, 43, 79
Lushey, C. & Munro, E.   19, 23, 24, 25, 26, 31, 32, 33, 40, 79

M

Mental ill-heath (also see CAMHS) 4, 30, 52, 89
Mentoring   45, 46, 52, 54, 56
Methodology   15, 20, 23, 26, 29, 50, 53, 79
Money   33, 48, 90
'Moving on'   10
Mutual-aid model   46

N

National Children's Bureau   46
NEET   44
Neglect   3, 11, 42

O

Ofsted   7, 17
Outcomes   ii, 2, 4, 6, 7, 10, 16, 19, 42, 46, 48, 52, 53, 75, 76, 78

P

Pathway Plans & planning   ii, 5, 6, 34, 40, 43, 48, 49, 54, 91
Participation   11, 12, 26, 39, 43, 78, 91
Peer research   19, 79, 80
Personal Advisor   5, 34, 48, 49, 51, 55, 56
Personal influences   25
Police   6
Poverty   1
Prince's Trust   46
Professionals   v, 8, 9, 11, 12, 21, 22, 35, 39, 42, 49, 51, 78

Q

Qualification   5, 10, 47
Qualitative data   2, 22, 25, 77, 80
Quantitative data   24

R

Recruitment strategy   23
Reflexivity   24, 25, 30
Relationships   4, 35, 42, 43, 44, 46, 51, 54, 55, 56, 88
Relevant child   4, 5
Resilience   4, 5

Resources ii, 12, 19, 21, 29, 33, 36, 37, 40, 41, 47, 49, 52, 53, 56, 75, 91, 93
Risk 4, 28, 38, 42, 45, 53, 78
Role model 36, 42, 56, 88

S

Safeguard 3
Screening 23
Self
  efficacy 8, 35
  esteem 6, 11, 35, 36, 39, 56, 88, 89
  identity 6
  harm 6, 30, 90
  isolate 32
  worth 33, 35
Sexuality 4
Skills ii, 9, 21, 29, 34, 35, 36, 41, 44, 45, 46, 47, 48, 52, 53, 54, 56, 88, 89, 93
Specialist services ii, 7, 53, 54, 55
Social care iii, 13, 15, 21, 22, 37, 39, 40, 52, 78
Social Care Institute of Excellence 21
Social exclusion 1, 7, 9, 53
Social networks 32, 43, 47, 51, 55, 89
Social services 39, 91
Social work iii, 2, 6, 9, 24, 41, 50, 54
Social workers vi, 6, 7, 19, 34, 44, 51, 55, 77
State, the 2, 3, 6, 7, 9, 44
Staying Close 54, 55
Staying Put 8, 13, 46, 47, 54, 55
Stein, M. ii, 1, 2, 3, 7, 8, 9, 10, 11, 13, 42, 44, 45, 52, 54
'Strugglers' 10, 54
Substance misuse 4, 75
Suicide 30, 75, 90
Supervision 50
'Survivors' 10, 54
Systematic review ii, 15, 18, 19, 21, 22, 41, 50, 51, 53

T

Tenancy 34, 44
Tenant Management Organisation (TMO) 47
Themes (sub & higher order) ii, 19, 27, 29, 34, 41, 50, 76, 77, 78, 79, 88
Theory 41, 50, 51, 76
Training 2, 4, 25, 40, 44, 56, 79, 80
Transition ii, 1, 3, 5, 7, 9, 10, 14, 15, 16, 17, 19, 22, 23, 24, 31, 33, 34, 41, 44, 50, 53, 54, 55, 75, 77, 78, 79, 80
Triangulation 26, 75, 79

U

Unemployment 4, 8, 10, 37, 42, 52, 75, 90, 93
United Nations Convention of the Rights of the Child 11
Universal Services 7, 52, 53
University (see education)
Utilised Studies 22, 36, 42, 43, 74

V

Validity 22, 41, 50, 79
'Victims' 10
Voice ii, 2, 11, 12, 14, 15, 17, 19, 24, 25, 26, 27, 29, 31, 41, 50, 51, 53, 54, 76, 78, 79, 88

W

Welfare 3, 15, 16, 44, 53, 78
Well-being 5, 30, 39, 43, 55, 75, 76
Workforce 36, 47

Y

Young People ii, v, 1, 2, 3, 4, 5, 6, 7, 8, 9, 10, 11, 12, 13, 14, 16, 24, 31, 32, 34, 35, 36, 37, 38, 39, 40, 41, 42, 43, 44, 45, 46, 47, 48, 49, 50, 51, 52, 54, 55, 56, 57, 75, 77, 78, 79, 91
Youth 49

Printed in Great Britain
by Amazon